Praise for

Organizing for the Creative Person

"Creative, time-tested techniques and helpful illustrations and anecdotes plus sound psychological advice. Well done!"

—Susan Silver, author of *Organized to Be the Best!*

"Understanding the role brain dominance plays in learning skills, especially learning organization skills, is an important breakthrough, especially for people who are chronically disorganized."

—Judith Kolberg, Director, National Study Group on Chronic Disorganization

"From the personal organization box to the not-to-do list, *Organizing for the Creative Person* provides specific steps to dig out from the clutter for those wallowing in an avalanche of paper."

—Peter Jeff, Steelcase, Inc.

Organizing
FOR THE
Creative Person

DOROTHY LEHMKUHL

AND

DOLORES COTTER LAMPING

Crown Trade Paperbacks New York

To my mother, Gertrude Gengler, who, at age ninety-four, is still my inspiration and strength. May God bless her and provide more mothers like her.
—Dorothy Lehmkuhl

To the memory of Percy "Mr. Bones" Danforth and my parents, Mother-Mary and "God-Help-Us-Andy" Cotter. May they all rest in peace—they sure deserve it!
—Dolores Cotter Lamping, C.S.W.

Copyright © 1993 by Dorothy Lehmkuhl and Dolores Cotter Lamping

Illustrations copyright © 1993 by Donald R. Taylor

Published by Crown Publishers, Inc., 201 East 50th Street, New York, New York 10022. Member of the Crown Publishing Group.

Random House, Inc., New York, Toronto, London, Sydney, Auckland

CROWN is a trademark of Crown Publishers, Inc.

Manufactured in the United States of America

Design by Leonard Henderson

Library of Congress Cataloging-in-Publication Data

Lehmkuhl, Dorothy.
Organizing for the creative person: right-brain styles for conquering clutter, mastering time, and reaching your goals / by Dorothy Lehmkuhl and Dolores Lamping.—1st. ed.
p. cm.
1. Time management. 2. Creative ability. I. Lamping, Dolores. II. Title.
HD69.T54L44 1994
650.1—dc20 93-14372 CIP
ISBN 0-517-88164-0

10 9 8 7 6 5 4 3 2 1

First Edition

CONTENTS

ACKNOWLEDGMENTS

Our heartfelt thanks:

To our agents, Barbara Lowenstein and Toni Lopopolo, who made a *mission* out of getting our book published.

To our editor at Crown, Peter Ginna, whose tactful suggestions helped us avoid mistakes. Working with him was a joy.

To our clients and students who have shared their struggles with us. We have at times created dialogue to make a point as clear as possible. Many vignettes are composites to preserve both confidentiality and authenticity. Although the names are fictitious, the struggles are real.

And our hats are especially off to the people who led the organizing movement back in the 1970s and early 1980s—people such as Stephanie Winston, Alan Lakein, Don Aslett, Dr. Dru Scott, sisters Pam Young and Peggy Jones, Sandra Felton, and others whose original books and seminars influenced us greatly and made it easier for everyone to get organized.

We also want to acknowledge Dr. Selwyn Mills and Max Weisser, M.S.W.; Jacquelyn Wonder and Priscilla Donovan; Thomas R. Blakeslee; and others who have written books pertaining to right- and left-brain dominance. (Names of books written by these and other authors can be found in our bibliography.)

In writing this book, we were ever mindful of the need to give credit where credit was due. Many of the books we have used as sources for our work touch on the same ideas, however. We read many of these books more than ten years ago, and have integrated their ideas into our personal lives and expanded upon them in our own unique way, so it has become impossible to credit every single idea. We readily admit that a great deal of our original organizing knowledge was based on learning through those books. We acknowledge that without the work done by outstanding individuals who have preceded us, this book could never have been written. Their work formed some of the steppingstones to our expertise, and we thank them for their contributions to society in general and to our work in particular.

We also wish to acknowledge individuals who reviewed our work and gave us valuable feedback: Chris Unwin, Shirley Brackett, Susie Shurr, Dr. Charles and Kaye Roth, James J. Brown, and others whose bits and pieces aided us.

And we wish especially to thank the following:

My significant other, Malcolm "Mac" Danforth, who has lovingly motivated, supported, and encouraged me in this project from beginning to end.

My three sons, John, Michael, and Jim, who have learned to do their own grocery shopping, cooking, laundry, and so on, while attending college full-time—so that Mom could work on this and other projects.

My coauthor, for her faith, determination, and perseverance in spite of obstacles.

—Dolores Cotter Lamping, C.S.W.

My family—Bruce, David, Scott, and Gregg—for their patience and understanding over the months and years it took to bring this project to fruition.

My coauthor, for her insightful contributions and attention to clarity.

—Dorothy Lehmkuhl

INTRODUCTION

"Come into my parlor . . ."
The spider wanted to invite the fly.
But he just couldn't say it
'Cause his web was all awry.

People often joke about disorganization, but jokes can be a screen for genuine discomfort—a way of covering up feelings of embarrassment or inadequacy.

For centuries, certain people have wondered why they had such a difficult time staying organized, while equally intelligent people around them seemed to have no trouble at all. Just being told *how* to get organized hasn't solved these people's problems because—although they may not be aware of it—inner obstacles prevent their use of standard organizing techniques.

Many wonderfully talented people have been able to create anything and everything—except order. Despite their many exceptional abilities, they have a hard time attending to details, keeping things where they belong, finding what they need, getting to places on time, following through on projects, and so on. As we'll explain in the second chapter, a tendency toward brain dominance or preference makes it difficult for some of them to get organized in the conventional ways.

If someone appears, outwardly, to be untidy or disorganized, that person's unique abilities and genius may be hidden, even from himself or herself. If you're one of those people, you may feel criticism acutely, and the resulting loss of respect from others may discourage you and damage your self-esteem. You may even perceive yourself as deficient. When you lose or forget something, you may ask yourself, "What's the matter with me?"

It's a vicious cycle, because this discouragement robs you of the physical and emotional energy needed to attack the job of dealing with the disorder.

WHO CAN BENEFIT FROM THIS BOOK

If you tend to be disorganized, but it doesn't bother you or the people around you, you don't need this book.

If, on the other hand, disorder presents continuing problems for you, we want to give you insights into what may be causing these difficulties and offer some tools that may be helpful.

Whether disorder is pervasive in your life or there is only one small aspect of organizing that you want to master, you'll benefit from learning why you have had difficulty overcoming obstacles and how to integrate new organizing skills into your lifestyle. You will also master skills to take renewed charge of your life, feel better about yourself, and be able to relieve tensions in your relationships through mutual understanding and acceptance.

If someone you live or work with suffers from chronic disorganization, you will benefit from our book by understanding what makes that person tick and learning better ways to work with him or her.

HOW THIS BOOK IS DIFFERENT

This book differs from standard organizing books in three significant ways:

First, it is intentionally designed to appeal to creative people. (By this we mean those with natural flair, imagination, and unconventional ways of doing things—and who very often experience organizational difficulties.)

Second, it delves more deeply into the reasons why some people have trouble with organization. Specifically, it focuses on the different ways the right and left hemispheres of your brain work. Scientific studies have shown that creativity resides in the right hemisphere of the brain. However, the right hemisphere lacks any concept of time, structure, or detail; these traits reside in the left brain. If you are "right brain dominant," you are likely to be a creative person—but you're also likely to have problems organizing. (We'll talk about this more in Chapter 2.)

Finally, it makes unconventional suggestions about how to organize. These unique ideas may seem strange to the naturally orderly person, but we know that most standard systems simply don't feel comfortable or don't appeal to the creative person.

Specifically, we'll help you learn ways

- to keep your papers so you can find them without losing them in a filing cabinet
- to use your time more effectively, so you'll have more time left for fun and creativity
- to overcome procrastination
- to be in better control of your life without becoming rigid
- to handle criticism

A WORD ABOUT US

Since 1981, Dorothy Lehmkuhl has been teaching time management and organizing through seminars, speeches, writing, and consulting.

Dolores Cotter Lamping is a Specialist in Psychology and Education, a Certified Social Worker and Licensed Professional Counselor who has done individual, group, and family counseling. She has also taught self-development to adults at several colleges.

For many years the two of us, in our separate careers, have observed people who had difficulty with their organizational skills, and who came to us for help on an ongoing basis after struggling unsuccessfully with their everyday habits. We have been able to help these people, but are aware that there are innumerable others who continue to struggle with organizational skills, and who have no one in their communities to whom they can turn for help. We have combined insights gained through right- and left-brain research with organizing techniques based on new knowledge about human behavior.

In writing this book we are reaching out to you with understanding, knowledge, and experience of what has worked for other people. Having worked extensively with people with organizational difficulties, we know the difference between realistic and unrealistic goals and expectations. Even though you may have struggled for many years, the situation is never hopeless.

You can succeed by allowing us to lead you one step at a time until you begin to see a difference in your life.

We can offer you all the *tools* you need to succeed, but our power ends at the last page of this book. It is up to you to *choose* whether or not to use these tools.

If you want to succeed, these are the powers that must come from *within you*:

- the DESIRE to change
- the BELIEF that the rewards will be worth your efforts
- the DECISION to persevere until you do succeed

Allow us to come into your life and work with you. We'd like to help.

1

FULFILLING YOUR DREAMS

If you don't know where you are going,
it doesn't matter which road you take.

Almost everyone wants to be well organized, yet that dream is continually elusive for some. Becoming organized is not something you can roll up your sleeves and "do" in an afternoon; it is an ongoing process. This chapter has been designed to assist you in getting in touch with the dreams you want to fulfill. The following chapters will help you learn how to assess your organizing style and how to go about making your dreams a reality.

The Power of Choice

Everyone has the power to take control of his or her life, but not everyone takes advantage of it. This is *the power of choice,* and it's the greatest power in the world. Your power of choice can be your most noble ally or your most fearsome enemy, depending on how you CHOOSE to use it. You use your power of choice every day of your life. You choose what to wear, what to do next, how much to eat, what to say, whether to agree or disagree with those around you; you are making choices all the time. Even when you are doing nothing, it's because you have *chosen* not to do anything.

How you are organized is also a result of the choices you make on a minute-by-minute basis. If you choose to file papers away when you're finished using them, you'll tend toward better organization. If you choose to leave papers lying on your desk when you're finished with them, you'll end up with piles of papers on your desk.

The Power to Succeed

You also have *the power to succeed*. Some people succeed and some don't, and the difference is in the choices they make. The people who succeed are the ones who make the right choices. At first glance that sounds logical—but wait a minute! How do you know what the right choices are?

By knowing what you want.

"But how do I know what I want?" you argue.

By thinking through what you value in life.

If you don't know where you are going, it doesn't matter what direction you take. We ask, *If you don't know what you want in life, how do you know what to do next?*

Floating Through Life

Do you just sort of float through life, grasping first one opportunity and then another? Imagine the seeds of a dandelion puff blown into the wind. Do you try to grab at all the seeds—with the majority of them quickly floating farther out of your reach? After you've run and run, chasing these whimsical opportunities, do you return breathless, with empty hands? If you identify with this image, you need to understand what is happening in your life. It's time to take stock of where you are and where you want to go.

Or perhaps you are well directed in certain areas of your life, but not in others. Many people tell us that at work, for instance,

---

KNOW WHAT YOU WANT

The first step toward achieving success is figuring out what will make you, as an individual, feel successful. Knowing your goals then becomes your guideline on how to spend your time. If you don't know what you want, how do you know what to do next?

Do you find yourself chasing one opportunity after another?

they are able to focus on what they need to do almost perfectly, yet they exercise little or no direction in their personal lives.

Knowing what you want, and staking out a path that will get you there, *helps you make the right decisions about what to do next.* Rather than wildly pursuing many goals at once, focus on planning ahead. Consider carefully selecting cultivated seeds in order to create a flower garden of those dreams you most want to bring to full bloom.

Fantasizing for Success

One way of getting in touch with what you value in life is to fantasize for a minute. Picture yourself in the most perfect role you can imagine in your life:

- Are you a free-lance photographer?
- Have you earned your Ph.D.?

- Have you built a woodworking business that produces unique furniture?
- Are you the CEO of a gigantic Fortune 500 company?
- Are you free to go fishing anytime you want?
- Are you improving the world by joining an activist movement or doing grassroots community service?

Don't be limited by anything in your dreams—time, money, miles, age, or what you've been able or unable to do in the past. If you had unlimited amounts of skill, energy, materials, physical abilities, resources, and self-confidence, what would you do? How would you like to spend your time?

Visualize for a moment exactly how your home, office, or studio would look. Picture the inside and the outside. What would the setting be? How would it sound? What scents would prevail? Would you be alone or with others? Who would those others be?

Consider even more questions. When you die, what will you have wanted to accomplish? Will you be disappointed because you wanted to do some things that you didn't even try?

According to the noted psychiatrist Elisabeth Kübler-Ross, "I made a living but I never really lived" is the single most common regret of the terminally ill. Evaluate what "really living" means to you. Don't be confined by "limited thinking." (After all, a goal is nothing but a dream set within a time frame.) Someone has said, "Those who can see the invisible can do the impossible." If you can open up your mind to dream of *any* possibility, you will be less likely to look back with regret on missed opportunities.

When you have carefully thought about the above, you are well on your way to goal-setting—to making choices that will aim you toward your success.

When we refer to success in this book, we are not necessarily talking about money or advancement—or even about being "perfectly" organized. Success means whatever you want it to mean. It means accomplishing whatever you want out of life. It's all right not to consider material wealth as having paramount importance in your life. In fact, we believe those who choose not to chase after unending wealth are more content than those who do. What is important is that you build your own castles in the air, whatever they may be, and strive to make them real. A Spanish proverb says, "If you build no castles in the air, you build no castles anywhere." So castles in the air are fine—wonderful, in fact. But if you want them to last, you must build a foundation under them, or they will be gone with the wind.

Setting out your goals in writing provides the foundation for ensuring the permanence of your castles in the air. Laying that foundation will give you a picture of your future. Whether you dream of becoming a famous surgeon or artist, or of starting your own business, you will become the person in your dreams if you lay a solid foundation and build on it.

Others' Expectations

You will never achieve true success—that is, a deep feeling of satisfaction and contentment—if you only work to fulfill others' expectations. If you've been raised to take over the family business, for instance, but have little interest in the daily dealings of that company, you'll never be happy. Innumerable people have become doctors, lawyers, or ministers because it was a "family tradition," only to find that those medical, legal, or religious professions did not suit them. We are not suggesting, however, that you just walk away from present commitments without making alternative arrangements.

AVOID A ME-FIRST ATTITUDE

A me-first attitude at the expense of others will ultimately result in failure. You must take good care of yourself, but don't just walk away from current commitments. Remember that a truly successful life includes ethics, family, and community.

Do Activities to Achieve a Goal

You don't "do" a goal; that would be like "doing" a dream. A goal is something you achieve or accomplish. It's something you work toward, usually over a period of time, and it's achieved by doing a series of *activities.*

If you want to become a surgeon, for instance, your activities would include researching what premedical courses would be necessary, which schools would be best, applying to the schools, taking the required courses, and so on. Someday, after completing all those activities, you would indeed accomplish your goal of being the surgeon of your dreams.

The person with little foresight—one who tends to "live for today"—will have difficulty sticking with doing the necessary activities to achieve a goal. For example, it's sometimes difficult for this person to see how saving money on small, out-of-pocket expenses today can help toward starting a much-wanted business in the distant future. This is one of many reasons for putting your goals in writing. Keeping an eye on your goals helps motivate you to complete the activities that will achieve them.

"It's Too Late"

You may think you're too old to realize your dreams. "That may be fine for younger people," you say, "but I'm too old for all that now." Perhaps that's true—and perhaps it's not. Although you may not reach the degree of success you visualized in years past, it's usually working toward your goal that brings true satisfaction. Consider some of the following:

> A woman in her late thirties, with a family, applied for medical school. When the counselor reminded her she would be forty-four years old when she graduated, she replied, "Sir, God willing I'll be forty-four years old anyway, and when I get there I'd rather have that degree in my hand."

> An eighty-three-year-old woman graduated from a college in Michigan. During her schooling she worked

four hours a day, five days a week, and overcame a heart attack and breast cancer.

An eighty-year-old Michigan woman rode 2,800 miles on her motorcycle during 1989. "Honda Honey," as she is known, also snowmobiles and water-skis, which she took up at age fifty-seven. "Don't just sit and relax," she said. "Take the challenge."

IT'S NEVER TOO LATE

Just because you're advanced in years doesn't mean you are too old. Even the elderly wear braces on their teeth, get college degrees, take swimming lessons, and start new careers. (Accept the fact, however, that your goals may change as your life experiences change.)

Take Credit

Although you need to reach for the stars, don't set impossible goals. You can't regrow an arm or move an ocean. Trying to attain the impossible only sets you up for failure. If you take an oath to lose ten pounds in one week, you may end up starving yourself and still probably lose only six pounds. (And at the end of the week you may binge on food because you are so hungry). Once more you'll be down on yourself because you feel you'll never attain the goals you set for yourself.

Instead, keep your feet on the ground by setting small, attainable goals. By doing a little at a time, you can feel successful. Before you know it, these little steps will add up to incredible achievements. Instead of going for ten pounds, decide to lose one or two pounds a week for five weeks. Then, if you end up losing only four pounds during that time, give yourself credit for losing that much. Rather than considering yourself a failure for not losing ten, realize you made worthwhile progress and you are four pounds lighter than when you began. That's success!

Set realistic goals, and give yourself credit for accomplishing them.

CHANNELING YOUR EFFORTS

Now that you understand the importance of making choices, why you need to know what you want in life, and what goal-setting will do for you, it's time to consider which of your many dreams are most important to you. Let's say that as the most important things in your life you have chosen to make money, to have a quality family life, and to help others in the form of volunteer work.

Imagine that your efforts, energies, and opportunities fall in the form of rain, and you are standing in that rain holding an umbrella. Even though the raindrops are abundant, you aren't catching any of them.

But suppose that underneath the edges of the umbrella is a circle of buckets. As you stand holding the umbrella perfectly straight, most of the raindrops fall off the edges down into the empty pails, with some falling in between.

If these buckets have no purpose, they will have no meaning for you, and the opportunities represented by the raindrops will be wasted. So let's label three of these pails "Making Money," "Family," and "Helping Others." If you want to focus on only three buckets (goals), you can tilt your umbrella so that the greatest amount of rain will fall into those three pails.

Now think about the activities you can do in order to make money. Envision a different set of buckets beneath another umbrella. Imagine taking your "Making Money" bucket and pouring it out over the second umbrella. You have labeled this second set of buckets with possible ways to make money. Perhaps one is labeled "College," representing going back to college to get a degree in interior decorating; another might be "Sales," for going into a new sales position; yet another might be "Present Position," for staying in your present occupation and figuring out ways to earn more money there, and so on.

Try to channel your efforts to make the most of your opportunities.

You have the power to tilt your second umbrella at will to direct the "rain" from your "Making Money" bucket into whichever surrounding buckets you choose.

Some of your energies and opportunities will still fall into the other buckets or onto the ground between the buckets, which is okay, because no single bucket can contain all the opportunities that will come your way. You must learn to be comfortable letting some of life go by while you concentrate on what is important to you. You need to choose which buckets to fill, focus on them, and not be concerned with the rest.

Maybe this umbrella/bucket vision will give you a graphic idea of why you need to make choices among your "buckets" or goals. Once again, catching just a little rain in many buckets or opportunities, or putting just a little energy or effort into a wide variety of things, may net you very little in the long run. While the rain of energy and opportunities is prolific, it is not unending.

Record Your Goals

One of the basic elements of successful goal setting is recording your fantasies in some way. Capture every idea you come up with, no matter how silly it may seem. Be *unlimited* in your thinking.

Put down everything you can imagine you might ever want to accomplish. Don't be limited by *anything*—time, money, geography, or past failures. Remember your childhood dreams and ask yourself if you would still like to try for some of them.

You can do this in one of several ways. First, you can make lists on one or more sheets of paper. This is the simplest and quickest way to proceed. If, however, you resist list-making and are artistic, perhaps you would rather draw pictures of your goals. Instead of writing many ideas on one paper, take a small sketch pad and do a rough drawing of each of your dreams on separate sheets. Use color markers to liven them up if you like, but we caution you not to get caught up in the act of drawing and become distracted from the task at hand. Your mission is to get all of your possible goals down on paper, not to see how well you can draw.

Another way to record your goals is to do that very literally—on an audiocassette. Keep your tape recorder handy, and each time you think of something else you'd like to do—whether it's a major project or a lifetime goal—push the Record button. In the same way as with a written list, you'll be able to save these ideas and listen to them again at will.

We hope you don't have an aversion to recording your goals in some manner. Some people are fearful of doing this because they feel that once their goals are written down, they are then putting themselves into the position of being "forced" to follow through—either by themselves or by others. They somehow have the feeling that once they're on paper they're written in concrete, and that if they don't achieve the goals, it's a sign of failure.

Please understand that goals are written in sand, not in concrete. Because interests, lifetime experiences, and personal situations change so rapidly in our society, there is no disgrace in changing your mind. You will be happier, however, if you can settle down to heading in one direction without constant changes. Perpetual changes in course will only lead you in circles.

Avoid sharing goals with someone who might not be positive about the goals or your ability to achieve them. If you're concerned about another person ridiculing you about your goals, then simply find a private place to keep your list—in the middle of a large unused book on your shelf, for instance. (Just don't forget where you put it! If that's a concern, write down the location.)

Prioritize

After you have recorded all your possible goals, begin making choices. By making a new list, forming separate piles of sketches, or listening to your tape, divide your list into classifications labeled *A, B,* and *C.*

You can take advantage of only so many opportunities in life. Be at least a little realistic while shooting for the stars. Whittle down your list to those few objectives that will make you, as an individual, feel most successful, and concentrate on those. In this case, *A* represents those ideas that have the highest priority, *C* the least important, and *B* in between. In making your decisions, it may help to ask yourself, "When I die, will I care if I have accomplished this goal?"

When you have finished separating your list into columns or your drawings into piles, use time-management expert Alan Lakein's method:

Separate all of your *B* items out of the *B* category and shift them either into the *A* or *C* sections, so no *B*'s are left. Then take the dreams in your *C* category and tuck them away to work on in the future, after you have achieved your more pressing needs. This leaves you only with *A*'s—the goals (or buckets) into which you want to pour your greatest energies.

If you are left with too many *A* goals—say eight or more—we suggest reprioritizing them in the same manner, subdividing them again into *A*, *B*, and *C* categories. This will assure you of being able to focus on what will help you feel most successful.

Don't be insecure about delaying some of the things you

Sort your priorities into A's, B's, and C's; then decide if those B's are really A's or C's.

want. So long as you are accomplishing other things even more important to you, the rest will still be awaiting your attention.

Creating a Time Frame

Setting goals is just great—but if you want your dreams to come to fruition, you need to devote some time to achieving them. For that reason it is imperative to consider when you want to devote that time to achieving your goals. You may remember that earlier in this chapter we mentioned that goals are merely "dreams set within a time frame." The time frame will help keep you on track. We recommend that you write next to each of your goals the date by which you would like to achieve that goal. This will be discussed in more detail in later chapters.

Once again, you aren't writing this date in permanent ink. It's changeable, but you have to start somewhere, so write down a time that you think would be acceptable to achieve your goal.

Congratulations! *You have now identified the most important objectives in your life.*

Now that you understand which roads you want to choose in order to follow your dreams, the following chapters will be devoted to helping you make those dreams come true.

SUMMARY

- *Your organizing style is a result of the choices you make on a minute-by-minute basis.*
- *The first step toward success is figuring out what will make you as an individual feel successful.*
- *Knowing what you want helps you make the right decisions about what to do next.*
- *Through visualizing, get in touch with what you value.*
- *Don't be afraid to dream the impossible dream.*
- *Success means accomplishing whatever you want out of life, not living up to others' expectations.*
- *Goals are achieved by doing a series of activities.*
- *Put the most energy and effort into those goals you most want to achieve.*
- *Record your goals in some way—on a tape recorder, in writing, or in pictures.*
- *For the excitement of seeing your dreams come true, set up a prioritized schedule or time frame.*

2

ASSESSING YOUR ORGANIZING STYLE

Your Style—Arbie or Elbie

Like fingerprints, each person's organizing style is unique. At one end of the spectrum, you may be extremely well organized, with your own brand of neatness and order prevailing in every aspect of your life. In that case, your desk has no papers on it, your clothing, home, car, and children are perfect. And you may feel very tired. You may also feel very critical of others who do not live up to your organizational standards.

At the other extreme, of course, are people who have difficulty with every aspect of organization. In that case, you may retain jumbled piles of papers on your desk, never throw things away, leave a trail of clutter wherever you go, and feel a total lack of concern about time commitments. You may also harbor feelings of guilt and shame because you've been criticized so often by others who wish you were more organized.

Few people exactly fit either of these extremes, of course. No doubt you'll fall somewhere in between, by exhibiting your own unique blend of behaviors—some on the well-organized side, some not.

Even though fingerprints are all different, the FBI still classifies them into broad categories. In the same way, organizing styles can also be broadly categorized. For the purposes of this book, we will separate organizing styles into just two categories:

Left-brain dominant. These people, whom we'll call LBs or "Elbies" for short, tend to be tidy, methodical, and punctual—"well organized" in the standard sense.

Right-brain dominant. RBs, or "Arbies," are characteristically creative, but their traits are the opposite of those of left-brain-dominant persons.

Right- and Left-Brain Dominance

To understand these two categories, it's necessary to understand what we mean by right- and left-brain dominance.

The name that stands out above all others in split-brain research is that of Dr. Roger W. Sperry of the California Institute of Technology. He was awarded the Nobel Prize in 1981 for his work on the two hemispheres of the brain. Since then, a great deal more research has broadened our knowledge of split-brain thinking.

In brief, it has been found that everyone uses both sides of the brain simultaneously, but each hemisphere serves distinctly different functions. While some people use each side almost equally, most people naturally depend more on one hemisphere of their brains than on the other. This is called *dominance* or *preference* (because the person prefers to live, act, or think in certain ways). As a shortcut, we'll refer to the right hemisphere of the brain sometimes as the "right brain," and to the left hemisphere as the "left brain."

While the right brain produces a broad spectrum of intuitive and creative talents, the left brain produces those talents necessary for traditional organizing skills. It's only natural, then, that people who prefer right-brain activities will have developed more right-brain skills and may not have concentrated their efforts as much on learning left-brain organizing skills.

Understanding the Different Styles

Understanding different styles can help explain human behavior, which affects success and personal contentment and in turn directly affects our self-esteem and relationships with others. This chapter will help you discern your own unique organizing style and begin to give you insights about why you and others around you exhibit certain habits; it will give you a capsule version of the characteristics of each hemisphere of the brain, with emphasis on the right hemisphere. Many other traits will be more fully described throughout the book.

As you read these pages, keep remembering that every reader will identify with a different combination of characteristics. One person may be acutely aware of time (a left-brain, or Elbie, trait), for instance, yet have difficulty dealing with clutter (a right-brain, or Arbie, trait). Another reader may be well balanced; that is, he or she may identify with an almost equal number of traits from each hemisphere of the brain, but lack self-discipline. A third might identify strongly with such left-brain traits as analyzing money matters, yet also manifest strong right-brain behaviors, such as a vivid imagination. We think you'll smile with recognition as you identify your own idiosyncrasies.

As we begin to draw a word-picture of an Arbie, we wish to emphasize that for balanced living, *right-brain skills are as essential as those of the left brain.* Most right-brain-dominant people have developed a profusion of organizing skills and function beautifully in most aspects of their lives.

As organizing pioneer and author Stephanie Winston told us, "Corporate chief executives are generally considered to be 'creative' rather than 'analytical' types, yet every single one of the approximately twenty-four corporate chief executives I spoke to for a study I conducted was not only organized, but *extremely* organized, both in their personal practices and in their office practices." In other words, even though these executives may well have been natural Arbies, they had recognized the importance of left-brain skills and had worked hard to develop them, also.

Every one of these people makes significant contributions to society through his or her intuitive and creative approaches to life.

The purpose of our book, however, is to discuss various *undeveloped* skills and/or behaviors and how, even if they don't come naturally, you can develop them.

Chris: Portrait of an Arbie

This Arbie is a well-known graphic artist now, but things weren't always so easy for him.

Chris is a highly talented person who is highly attuned to the *feeling* of life. When music plays, he *feels* it;
when someone has a problem, it's easy for him to em-
pathize. He's creative at "brainstorming" ideas, and has
innovative artistic talents. He's a colorful storyteller,
loves to improvise, delights in having fun, and has a rich
imagination.

Chris had a hard time on his job, however. He used to
work for a large corporation until he became too unhappy. The work wasn't difficult, but it required a kind
of structure that he hated. He had to be at his desk at
8:00 A.M. sharp. He was expected to keep his filing in
accordance with company procedures. His work had to
be exact, and the corporation was not lenient with people who lost papers or missed deadlines.

Finally, feeling like a failure, Chris quit his job and
opened a small business of his own, a design firm serv-
ing businesses. He began creating logos, brochures, attractive sales flyers, and any other artwork he could
find, on a contractual basis. Although his customers
were extremely pleased with his designs, he was barely
scraping by financially. However, he relished his work
and would have loved it if he could spend every waking
moment doing what he did best.

Unfortunately, other tasks beckoned strongly. As his
business grew, so did the piles on his desk. Art supplies
were strewn across the studio. He had more and more
trouble finding the information he needed when customers called. His bank account hadn't been reconciled
for months, and it was accidentally overdrawn several
times. He'd filed two applications for extensions on his
income tax, and was feeling overwhelmed when he
called on us for help.

"You exhibit traits that would lead us to believe you're
right-brain dominant," we told Chris.

"Oh, you don't have to tell me!" he said. "I already
know what's wrong with me."

"That's the point we're trying to get across to you,

Chris," we said. "There's *nothing* wrong with you! The way you act and the things you do are completely normal, and there's nothing wrong with being an Arbie or acting like one. It's not wrong, but merely *different from* the organizing styles of left-brain-dominant people."

"Are you telling me that after all my troubles on my job, there's nothing wrong with me?" he asked, perplexed.

"That's exactly what we're saying," we responded. "In fact, we think it was the corporation that missed out by not recognizing your wonderful talents and allowing you to make the significant contributions you were obviously so capable of making."

At that point we could actually see the tension and depression dissolving from his face. Instead of feeling ashamed, he realized that his "problem" was merely that he possessed a different organizing style. As he began to assimilate this one important fact, it slowly dawned on him that this single insight had great implications for the rest of his life.

Getting organized and staying that way is still not easy for him, but now Chris has a more balanced perspective about his abilities. We helped him to see that by nature he was more concerned with moods, feelings, images, and holistic thinking than with clutter and details, and that organizational techniques consistent with his right-brain dominance were available to him.

Rather than being distracted by negative thoughts about what a "failure" he is, he is now better able to concentrate on what needs to be done. With newfound confidence, he is gradually developing his left-brain skills.

We taught him how to make better use of his time; how to keep his desk neater, with his papers and other materials stored in such a way that he can always find what he needs and yet is natural for him to use; and how to contract out some of the work that's more difficult for him.

Ironically, even though he's spending a little more time on

organizational activities, he now actually has *much more* time left over to spend on creative ideas, because he uses the rest of his time more judiciously. He has now built a reputation as an innovative creator of graphic arts—and, of course, he has become more successful financially, as well.

We wrote this book for people like our client Chris, people who have tried hard over many long and difficult years to get organized, but who have never felt successful at overcoming this vexing problem. Not only have they been unable to "get it all together," but they've had to live with the constant condescending and critical comments from others who command "better" ways of doing things.

THE RIGHT BRAIN

In order to understand why people have different organizing styles, it's necessary to understand the workings of the right and left hemispheres of the brain.

The right brain has its own unique way of dealing with information. It is sometimes referred to as the unconscious mind (although this is technically incorrect), but because the right brain has no language ability, it can't verbalize its thinking processes. Rather, its thinking is formed in a rapid, complex, and spatial manner, sometimes in the form of dreams.

Right-brain processes are difficult to explain because they are by nature nonverbal, abstract, holistic, simultaneous, and unlimited in any way. Unless the left brain is informed of the vivid images or irrational sequences of events experienced by the right brain, they remain unspoken even to the person who has them, and are therefore considered by some to be below the conscious level.

Although not expressed verbally, the right brain's consciousness can be expressed in body language, in actions, or in various art forms. One preschool girl drew a picture on a piece of paper. When asked what the picture represented, she replied, "It's a picture of a thought." This was something she had created in her right brain; she saw no need to identify it.

Dancing with free-flowing body movements to the rhythm of music would be another example of this nonverbal expression.

Right-brain-dominant people—some of whom are Arbies—are the people we might call artists in the generic sense, since the right brain deals with such aspects of human life as music, images, colors, face and pattern recognition, and so on.

Though the potential for creative and/or artistic pursuit is greater for the right-brain-dominant person, that doesn't mean all Arbies are artists or use their creative or artistic skills in their workaday world—*and it certainly doesn't mean that "all creative people are messy."* As we've stated before, many creative people have highly developed organizing skills and should never be automatically categorized as disorganized simply because they enjoy great creative abilities.

Still, right-brain tendencies do contribute in shaping an Arbie's view of the world. Although Chris was not employed as an artist while he worked for the corporation, his natural instincts were more attuned to *global concepts* than to detail work.

Round Pegs, Square Holes

The effects of being right-brain dominant become evident during childhood. Traditionally, elementary schools have provided little training for right-brain creativity. Although education is changing, in the past the talents of right-brain people went largely unappreciated in schools, and teaching methods were geared toward the left-brain-dominant person. When he was a child, Chris's artistic and creative abilities far exceeded his fellow students' abilities, yet that fact was ignored. The left-brain children received high marks for left-brain skills such as writing and arithmetic, while Chris was made to feel a failure.

There has been good reason for the emphasis on left-brain activity, however. In our society, adults are thrust deeper and deeper into a left-brain world. As Stephanie Winston's study suggests, success in the corporate and private world absolutely requires left-brain skills. These include the abilities to set and work toward specific goals; to handle papers, money, and accounting procedures including taxes, insurance, banking, and government forms; to analyze accounts and long-range business planning; to manage time well; and on and on.

Also, the corporate world traditionally adheres to a narrow organizational structure. Although, as with education, the corporate culture is in transition, too often right-brain creativity and flexibility are still crushed by left-brain business people who adhere to logical, rational ways within the unwritten corporate culture.

Add to this the fact that Arbies are often personally disorganized, and you'll understand why people like Chris have a difficult time in life, sometimes feeling that they are round pegs trying to fit into the square holes of society.

Of course, a great deal more than just right- or left-brain dominance also goes into the making of each personality. Genetics, culture, education, and environment also greatly influence the development of every human being, and we do not mean to minimize their impact. Physical handicaps, short-term memory loss, and learning or attention difficulties, to name a few examples, can also affect organizational abilities. Our focus here, though, is on those hemispheric differences thus far explored through split-brain research.

Right-Brain Traits

One of the Arbies' greatest strengths lies in their giftedness in interpersonal relationships. They charismatically draw people to them, and with little effort they are successful at maintaining satisfying relationships on a long-term basis.

The right hemisphere perceives information globally, as a "total picture," so to speak. It produces emotion, images, intuition, sensuality, creativity, and humor. If you're an Arbie, you use the right hemisphere when you respond to poetry or metaphors, when you dream or have ideas, or when you draw a picture of your perceptions.

The Right Brain and the Senses

The right brain is *sensual*. You use it when you are listening to music or creating a sculpture, for instance. In fact, any uninhibited sensual behavior, such as making love, comes from that side. It reacts in a direct and primitive way to sensory information and therefore retains the emotional depth, power, and impact of the feelings at the gut level. This explains why Arbies normally express a lot of feeling. The left brain, by contrast, processes sensory experiences—sight, hearing, taste, touch, and smell—through words, thus losing much emotional value.

The right half of the brain helps you see the whole of what you perceive. You are using your right brain when you're looking at things as they are at the present moment. You see likenesses, you understand one thing as being a metaphor for another, you see relationships among the parts and how they fit together to form a whole. The right side of the brain is used to recognize and remember faces, and to respond to visual instructions.

Arbies

- frequently use metaphors and analogies in their speech
- are very responsive to emotional appeals
- deal simultaneously with several problems at once
- use their hands a lot in conversation

If you're an Arbie, you may tend to

- be playful in solving problems
- respond to things with emotion
- interpret body language easily
- have a good sense of humor
- process information subjectively
- improvise

Without the structure of the left-brain influence, Arbies tend to be casual, easygoing, "laid back," and fun-loving. They tend to react with feelings first.

The Unrestricted Right Brain

The Arbie has a very difficult time with limits. Given a choice, the typical Arbie would operate as if there were no limits on anything—time, money, calories, or energy—and certainly not on ideas. If you're an Arbie, you may act as if there were also no limits on how much clutter you can accumulate, for instance.

The same may be true of money. You may buy whatever you feel like buying, never stopping to figure out what it will do to your budget.

If you can't set limits for yourself, you may also have a hard time pacing yourself, expending huge amounts of energy in one area and then being totally depleted in another.

You may appear to your colleagues to have very high energy—both physically and emotionally—in your workplace. You may be a peak performer, and people may have the impression that you are that way all the time. However, when you go home each night you may walk in the door, head straight for the couch, and *collapse*. Your husband or wife may wonder if he or she is married to someone who is comatose, because you may be in that state most of the time at home. Learning to pace yourself can be a giant first step toward avoiding difficulties and leading a more balanced life.

The right brain can be very inspirational and attuned to spiritual things, as well as highly sensual. Nobody, however, would ever accuse Arbies of being practical, as logic is produced in the opposite hemisphere.

Even the way Arbies describe things differs sharply from Elbies' descriptions. For example, asked to close your eyes and describe the place where you are now, you may say it's large, comfortable, warm, and so on. Since Arbies tend to process information in an overall sensory way, you will describe your *sensations* as you experience that room.

The Right-Brain Thought Sequence

The characteristic Arbie thought sequence when acting on an idea is

FEELING→ACTION→ANALYSIS

The way in which this process is utilized profoundly affects the organizing style of the individual.

For example, one warm, sunny day you might suddenly get

a yen (idea) to go to the beach. Loving spontaneity (feeling), you may gleefully drop whatever you're doing and head for the water's edge (action). Only after you've spent half a day there and gotten sunburned will you realize (analysis) you failed to bring along suntan lotion. Upon your return, you might also remember that you've failed to cancel some appointments, thereby affecting both you and others. Despite the negatives, however, you will still have enjoyed the trip immensely, and will later reflect on it with humor and zest.

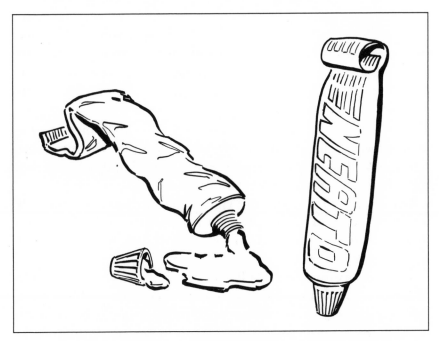

Your toothpaste tube may tell you whether you're an Elbie or an Arbie.

The Toothpaste Tube

If you're still wondering whether you're right-brain dominant or not, just for the fun of it we'll mention what is probably the most universal of all indicators of your organizing style: your tube of toothpaste!

Arbies don't care at all whether the tube is squeezed at the bottom, the middle, or the top, and the cap of the toothpaste seems to serve no purpose at all; once it's been removed, it will never be used again.

If you identify with this trait, then you are probably an Arbie, because this is one part of your life in which you are most likely to act naturally, rather than in more public aspects of your life.

THE LEFT BRAIN

The left brain thinks in sequential order, and processes certain kinds of reasoning:

logic	structure
discipline	detail
analysis	sequence
time orientation	language

The verbal-oriented, left-brain behaviors of Elbies are exactly the opposite of those of Arbies. People who predominantly use their left hemispheres are logical and rational, but may show little emotion or humor.

Just as Chris had a natural right-brain preference, there are many other people who prefer a highly structured, left-brain lifestyle and who are even uncomfortable with humor, creativity, or emotion.

The organizing style of Elbies is entirely different from that of Arbies, too. Take clothing, for instance. Extreme left-brain dominants treat their clothing carefully; it would be beneath their dignity to be careless with them. They place their pants and coats and shirts on hangers in specific sections of their closets, neatly fold their underwear and sweaters in drawers or on shelves, make sure their earrings or cufflinks are stored together in an appropriate jewelry holder, and always put their soiled items into a hamper.

Saving junk is not a problem. Without emotion, left-brain people can easily—even icily—throw things out without blinking an eye (unless they are compulsively analytical). They have collections, but they will be well-thought-out selections of art, coins, or other categories, never just miscellaneous junk.

The Left-Brain Thought Sequence

The left-brain thought sequence is, predictably, the exact reverse of that of the opposite hemisphere. It is

ANALYSIS→ACTION→FEELING

Before Elbies proceed to take action on anything, they'll analyze the pros and cons (sometimes to death). If the idea is deemed logical or practical, they'll consider all the consequences, plan, and perhaps even talk themselves out of doing it before even getting started! Only when action is completed, however, will they appreciate the feelings gained from it.

For instance, a left-brain man might also get a notion (idea) to go to the beach. Instead of just jumping in the car and taking off as an Arbie might do, however, he will typically begin enumerating in his mind (analysis) the plans it will take to go off on this fun trip. He'll want to call others to accompany him, cancel other plans, grab flotation equipment, load up on sunscreen, pack a little snack, ice down some beverages, and bring an extra change of apparel, "just in case" (action).

Only after he has settled into his own spot in the sand will he begin to relax and enjoy the adventure (feeling). (Unfortunately, the best part of the day may be past by then.)

Left-Brain Verbal Attributes

In describing a room, instead of commenting on the feelings it elicits, an Elbie would give a very accurate, precise description of the room itself. He or she would analytically and logically tell how many pictures were on the walls, and would describe the style and color of the walls, furniture, flooring, lighting, and so forth—in such detail that someone who had never seen the room could easily picture it.

Criticism of Left-Brain-Dominant People

As you can see by the foregoing, in the same way that the right brain produces functions crucial to our everyday living, the left brain complements its opposite hemisphere by utilizing the other half of the brain's capabilities. Criticism of Arbies will be discussed throughout this book; we feel, however, that Elbies should receive "equal time" and also be aware of criticism that tends to come their way.

When people depend too much on left-brain abilities and resist utilizing the opposite side, they may overdo the positive aspects of their abilities and turn them into negatives. Some complaints heard about extremely left-brain people are that they may be too

controlling	impatient
concrete	judgmental
critical	"cheap"
cautious	obsessive
pristine	robotlike
insensitive	compulsive
rigid	boring

They may also be told that they throw out valuable things and are always straightening up.

The Toothpaste Tube

As you've probably guessed, if you meticulously squeeze the toothpaste tube up from the bottom and carefully replace the cap each time it's used, you are most likely left-brain dominant.

How the Two Hemispheres Work Together

Although the left hemisphere seems devoid of emotion, it takes over when you need to analyze or plan something step by step, when you need to speak, be logical, or figure something out, or when you need to be objective. The right brain is also good at some things and not so good at others. If you're an Arbie, others may envy your creativity, sensuality, spontaneity, or intuition, but other things that come naturally to a left-brain-dominant person may be more difficult for you.

For example, since the right brain has no sense of time, you may tend to lose track of how long you've been immersed in your activities, and get so involved in what's going on in the here and now that you don't plan ahead. Right-brain consciousness is, however, accessible to the left brain, where it can be interpreted and put into words and then expressed. Also, the right brain doesn't categorize or analyze, so it's very subjective. Such behaviors may cause problems in your daily life—either for yourself or in your relationships with other people.

Again, unless one hemisphere of a person's brain is totally dead, everyone utilizes both sides of the brain interactively. An interesting story is told about a neurosurgeon who, in the nineteenth century, performed an autopsy on a lawyer, and found that the right hemisphere of the man's brain was completely atrophied. He had never had the use of that side of his brain in his entire adult life, and most people had never noticed the difference. There are a lot of people walking around out there who might cause you to wonder if their right brains are similarly atrophied. Our concern here is not really with that problem, however.

A Quick Quiz: Are You an Arbie?

If you're still not sure which side of your brain you use predominantly, try taking the following quiz. The questions may help you understand yourself a little bit better. This is not a scientifically standardized test, but simply an informal self-awareness tool that we use with our clients. Don't spend time analyzing your answers, but just quickly circle either A or B, according to your initial reaction.

1.   A. Time often passes without my noticing.
      B. I am very aware of time.

2.   A. It's important for me to have everything where it belongs.
      B. As long as I can find what I need, I don't really care where things are kept.

3.   A. I follow my hunches and go with the flow.
      B. I analyze whether ideas are good or not before taking action.

4.   A. When speaking or writing, my natural inclination is to stick to the point.
      B. When speaking or writing, I tend to be free-flowing and creative, not feeling as though I must rigidly adhere to any specific guidelines.

5.   A. I like to do things spontaneously.
      B. I like to be deliberate and plan out what I'm going to do.

6.   A. Before my weight gets out of control, I impose limits on my eating and drinking habits.
      B. I eat whenever I feel like it and don't worry about it unless things get completely out of control, such as my weight, blood sugar, or cholesterol.

7.   A. I prefer to have my papers filed away.
         B. I like to keep my papers out in piles where I can see them.

8.   A. I file things by subject.
         B. I prefer to locate papers by color-coding.

9.   A. People criticize me for always running late.
         B. People criticize me for being too impatient.

10.   A. I like to throw things out when I don't need them.
         B. I like to save things in case I might need them.

11.   A. If other people's stuff is in my way, I climb over it.
         B. I get irritated when others don't adhere to my standards of neatness.

12.   A. It's hard for me to take time to play.
         B. If I want to do it, I want to do it *now*, and I don't want anyone to spoil my fun, even though I may regret it later.

To determine your score:

- Count all the A's of even-numbered questions and all the B's of odd-numbered questions, and add them together. These are "Elbie" points.
- Count all the A's of odd-numbered questions and all the B's of even-numbered questions and add them together. These are "Arbie" points.

The two sets of numbers should total 12.

If your score is 5 to 7 on either side, this suggests *well-developed skills on both hemispheres* of your brain, and therefore well-balanced thinking.

Scores of 8 to 12 Elbie or Arbie points suggest greater preference for one hemisphere. The higher your score on either side, the greater your preference for that hemisphere.

The preceding quiz does not provide a totally accurate assessment, but simply gives you an indication of your tendencies. While it probably didn't tell you anything about yourself that you didn't already know, it can confirm or clarify the awareness you already have of yourself.

This book is not intended as a scientific report on the many brain functions. What's important for our purposes is to explain the effects of right- or left-brain dominance on your organizational skills, and help you become aware of the resulting implications for your life and your relationships with others who exhibit different organizing styles.

SUMMARY

- *Organizing styles can be broadly divided into two categories: left-brain and right-brain modes.*
- *Self-understanding affects self-esteem and relationships with others.*
- *All people use both sides of the brain—but most people have a dominant or preferred side.*
- *Everyone has the capacity to develop his or her less fully developed side.*
- *In spite of criticism of Elbies, organizing styles instinctively used by right-brain persons are not wrong, just different.*
- *Time devoted to organizing is time gained, not time lost.*
- *Success in the corporate and private world requires left-brain skills.*

3

FOCUSING IN ON YOUR VISIONS

Each of us has an inner clock that started on the day we were born and will stop on the day we die. We don't know when that day will come, of course, but we do know that time, once past, can never be reclaimed, so it's incumbent upon us to make the most of our time until then.

The way you spend your time is the way you spend your life. How you decided to spend your time in the past has produced your present environment—where you are in life today. Your situation ten years from now will be the direct result of the way you spend your time between now and then. Therefore, consciousness of time and how you spend it directly affects the *quality* of your life.

Humans depend on the left hemispheres of their brains for their concept of time, its limitations, and all its associated connotations. Left-brain-dominant people have an awareness of time, all the time. They wear wristwatches, put clocks in strategic places, and keep track of time. They rarely run late.

The right side of the brain, however, has no concept of time whatsoever. Hence, if you are a right-brain-dominant person without interest in time, you may experience various difficulties. For example, you may arrive late at appointments. You may become engrossed in reading or whatever you're doing, and be unaware of the passage of time. You might not wear a watch—in fact, you may not care much about time and would be happier if clocks didn't exist.

Unfortunately, the real world doesn't allow people to function at their own speed, or make allowances for the fact that Arbies have their own built-in time frame. This conflict produces stress for those who are not attuned to time because it's unnatural for them. They'd prefer to follow their natural instincts—to live by their own rhythms—rather than to meet the demands of society by adhering to rigid schedules.

If living by the clock causes you stress, this chapter may give you a better understanding of why you handle time not wrongly, but differently from the way Elbies do, as well as help you make better use of it.

Choices

Your use of time is a prime example of your power of choice. You are perpetually making choices on a minute-by-minute basis. You may not be conscious of the fact that you are making a choice when you put a file away or leave it out, wash the dishes or stack them, or work on disliked tasks or not. You are even choosing whether or not to agree with what you're reading right now.

The question is, are you *aware* you are choosing freely to do what you are doing? Too many people feel they have no choices in life, that they are trapped in their circumstances. The fact is, you don't *have* to do anything. The following story illustrates our point.

Before he left his corporation, Chris was suffering terribly from burnout on his job, and he lamented to his wife almost daily how he wished he could quit soon. He was finally offered a "buyout," but then learned he could obtain much greater benefits by working just one more year, so he freely chose to stay on his job longer. Even though he still wasn't happy, he immediately noticed a difference in his own attitude about the pressures of his job. Instead of *having* to do the work, Chris now realized that he was choosing to stay on of his own volition, which removed some of his stress and made working that one extra year more agreeable.

This chapter is devoted to helping you make the right choices for you. The following three exercises may help evaluate where you stand today in this regard:

Exercise 1. What Do You Cherish Most?

Pause for a moment and think about what three things in your life you value, or that are more important to you than anything else. Write them below:

1. _____
2. _____
3. _____

You've indicated the things that you believe are most important to you. But are you spending your time in a way that reflects their importance? The answer may be eye opening.

Exercise 2. The 168-Hour Plan

Let's look at how you spent your time last week. There are 168 hours in seven days, so consider how you used them. Jot down how many hours you spent in each category below:

Personal life	Hours
Sleeping/eating	_____
Grooming/hygiene	_____
Driving or riding	
personal errands	_____
shopping	_____
traveling to and from work	_____
Exercising	_____
Cleaning/maintenance	_____
Talking in person	
to family/friends	_____
on personal business	_____
Talking on the phone	
to family/friends	_____
on personal business	_____

Mail/personal business   _____
Volunteering   _____
Praying/meditating   _____
Studying/reading   _____
Relaxing/watching TV   _____
Thinking/worrying/planning   _____
Other   _____

Business life   Hours

Planning/research   _____
Paperwork/computer   _____
Talking to co-workers   _____
Appointments/meetings   _____
Clients/customers/patients   _____
Phone calls   _____
Production   _____
Other   _____
                Total: 168 hours

Ask yourself these questions:

- Was it hard to remember how you spent your time?
- Did you take any time out this past week just for yourself?
- How many things did you do that you planned to do?
- How many things did you put off?
- What is it that you want to spend more time doing?
- What do you want to do less?
- Are you happy with the way you spent your time?

Now look back at how you spent the last 168 hours and ask yourself: *How many of those hours did I spend on those three things I listed that I cherish most?*

Exercise 3. Looking Back

As a final exercise, complete these two sentences:

- When I look at my life so far, I'm glad I took the time to

_____ .

- I regret I haven't taken the time to _____

_____ .

The past week—and each week—was a piece of your life. What you're doing with your time is what you're doing with your life. It would be a shame if week after week went by and you found you weren't devoting your time to what you cherish most.

When to Achieve Your Goals

If you're saying something is important in your life but you aren't spending time on it, then you need to change either what you say your values are, or the way you spend your time. Otherwise the result is frustration, guilt, or a great feeling of loss.

Kenneth Blanchard, Ph.D., coauthor of *The One-Minute Manager,* points out that it's important to manage the journey, not just announce the destination. You can't sit passively and wait for life to happen; you have to *make* it happen. You can have all the goals in the world, but if you want them to become reality, you need to act on them in meaningful ways to bring them about.

As we said earlier, goals are nothing more than dreams put within a time frame. So long as you don't decide when to achieve your greatest desires, they'll remain only that—dreams. It is therefore absolutely necessary that you decide when you'll start working on them, and set a target date for their completion. Without this critical decision, you may remind yourself relentlessly throughout a whole lifetime of a certain thing that would bring you great satisfaction, but until you actually set a time to begin working on it, it will always remain something just out of reach, something you're going to do "later."

ESTABLISH A TIME FRAME FOR YOUR GOALS

In writing, specify desired beginning, progress, and completion times for your goals. If you don't set aside specific times to work on them, your goals will remain only fantasies.

To Plan or Not to Plan

Success depends almost entirely on preparation. We found that out as children. Imagine two children racing windup toys. The toy that is given only a couple of quick twists won't go far. The child who takes the time to wind the toy to its limit, however, will win the race.

Because planning capacities (linear, step-by-step analysis) reside in the left brain, such planning can be unfamiliar and uncomfortable to those who depend primarily on their right brains. As a consequence, Arbies often avoid plotting a course before they begin a project.

The irony is that the less you plan, the higher your costs will be. The ultimate stress of failure incurred from *not planning* is greater than the original stress incurred by *doing the planning.* For instance, without planning to have the proper research available, a report may not be ready for a deadline; not planning study time properly for a test may result in a poor grade; not planning ahead to have proper clothing for an event may prove embarrassing.

Sometimes learning this lesson takes many years of a person's life, with a great deal of wear and tear to show for it in the meantime.

Organizing Your Activities Around Your Goals

The first and foremost suggestion for good time management is *Organize your activities around your goals.* In other words, spend your time doing what you want to get done. Goal-setting (knowing what you want) and time management (spending your time judiciously to get what you want) are inextricably joined.

Focusing

People with numerous ideas tend to expend their efforts in a scattered pattern. Instead of focusing on just one or two good ideas, they go first in one direction and then in another, and end up accomplishing a little bit of everything but not much of anything. They start down too many roads without finishing their trip on any of them. The most important key to staying organized is the word *focus*. Being distracted from one thing to another without finishing things as you go is a sure way to fail.

FOCUS ON WHAT IS MOST IMPORTANT TO YOU

Too often we do busywork, and then wonder where our time went and what we achieved. Resist the urge to do the next thing your eyes see; instead, let your brain guide you.

For instance, let's say you want to enroll in a time-management seminar that you know will help you work more effectively. You know today is the deadline for enrollment, because you've written it on your calendar. Instead of allowing incoming mail, current projects, and a thousand other little things to command your attention, make that one critical phone call. If you hadn't written that reminder on the calendar, you would have ended up letting it slip your mind after all, and allowing the deadline to pass. Give yourself credit for writing it down and encouragement for making the call.

Think of the word *focus* as an acronym:

$$F = Follow$$
$$O = One$$
$$C = Course$$
$$U = Until$$
$$S = Successful$$

Decide in advance which road you want to take, and then pursue it until you reach your desired destination.

It's all right to have several goals, but set aside realistic amounts of time to concentrate on each goal separately. This might be just fifteen minutes a day, one day a month, or two weeks a year. You can work on different goals at different times, but if you work on too many, all of your time will be taken up, with little achievement to show for any one of them.

Work on Your Highest Priorities First

The next time-management rule is to work on your highest priorities first, but let's clarify that statement before proceeding. The question is, how do you go about deciding what is your highest priority?

First, of course, you must know what your goals are, as we discussed earlier in this book. Then you must decide on the best way to go about achieving them—the task we are discussing here. Remember that selecting the best job is far more important than just doing any job to keep busy. Never confuse movement with action.

There are many popular ways to go about prioritizing your work, most of which would be difficult for Arbies to utilize. One of the more recent theories compares *urgent* tasks to *important* ones, and it may be of more use to Arbies than any other means of prioritizing.

Urgent Versus Important

Urgent is a word that signifies something that demands your immediate attention. It might be a project that's due today, a child crying, or a ringing telephone. Some things that are urgent are also important—a fire alarm or a summons to the boss's office. But others are not. That ringing telephone may just be a salesperson or a friend calling to gossip—something you can deal with later, or not at all.

Conversely, *important* tasks are those that will help you achieve your goals. Often these are not of an urgent nature, so they don't command your immediate attention. But if you keep putting them off until an "opportune" time—because you're too busy with "urgent" things—they may never get done.

For instance, you may want to take a course that would be important to make you more successful or to help you learn a new profession, but if you're "too busy" with "urgent" routine activities to take the time to attend classes, your life will continue exactly as it is now. Sorting out the important aspects of your life from urgent ones can turn your life around 180 degrees.

Without careful consideration, people are inclined to tackle their activities in the following order:

1. Urgent and important
2. Urgent but not important
3. Important but not urgent
4. Not urgent and not important

For you to achieve your dreams, however, numbers two and three above would need to be inverted. Let's look at this more closely.

1. Urgent and Important. This still has to be number one. A crying baby is both urgent and important—urgent because the child needs attention immediately, but also important because the welfare of your child must be high on your priority list.

This category represents emergencies, deadlines, and short-term goals. If, for instance, heavy equipment breaks down on a large construction project, making repairs overshadows the importance of other work because the costly equipment and workers are idled until it is fixed.

2. Important but Not Urgent. Attempt to spend your greatest amount of time doing work that falls into this category. Steven R. Covey advises this in his book *The Seven Habits of Highly Effective People*. The rationale is that when proper planning is done, crises and other urgent matters are virtually eliminated and work can be done in a *pro*active mode, rather than in a *re*active one. (*Proactive* means making things happen—the opposite of waiting until things happen, good or bad, and then reacting to them.) If you don't plan—and work—ahead, you're doomed to spend your time "putting out fires" instead of on more productive efforts.

3. Urgent but Not Important. This category is the greatest pitfall for most people. Things like telephone calls, informal visitors, mail, and in-box items all need to be assigned priorities. Just because something is in front of you doesn't necessarily mean it's worthy of your immediate attention.

Most spontaneous ideas will also fall into this category. Arbies need to be especially conscious of falling into the trap of spending long periods of time escalating urgent-seeming ideas that happen to cross their minds but that contribute little or nothing to their goals.

4. Neither Urgent nor Important. Finally, busywork and real time-wasters fall into this category. These are described elsewhere in this book, and might include unnecessarily perfectionistic work, or becoming immersed in reading junk mail.

As you can see in the illustration on page 47, tasks can fall into four quadrants corresponding to the above categories.

Effectiveness Versus Efficiency

Keep in mind that effectiveness, not efficiency, is the goal of good time management. You can do something efficiently, but if you're doing the wrong thing, it won't help you reach your goals. As author and consultant Tom Connellan says, "There's no point in doing well what you should not be doing at all."

URGENT VS. IMPORTANT

A. - URGENT and IMPORTANT	B. - IMPORTANT / NOT URGENT
Crises Deadline-Driven Projects Pressing Problems	Planning Production Prevention New Opportunities Relationships Recreation DAILY MAINTENANCE
C. - URGENT / NOT IMPORTANT	X. - NOT IMPORTANT / OR URGENT

Interruptions
Pressing Matters
Popular Activities
Some: Mail
     Reports
     Meetings
     Calls
	Trivia
	Busywork
	Timewasters
	Enjoyable Activities
	Some: Calls
	     Mail

List Your Own Activities in the Appropriate Squares Below:

A. - URGENT and IMPORTANT	B. - IMPORTANT / NOT URGENT
C. - URGENT / NOT IMPORTANT	X. - NOT IMPORTANT / OR URGENT

(Adapted from the work of Stephen R. Covey, Ph.D.)

Go back over the list of your activities in the last week and categorize each action into the chart on page 47 to see if you are spending your time appropriately. Then match your values with your highest priorities and clarify what does or does not bring fulfillment to your life in the long term.

SUMMARY

- *How you spend your time is how you spend your life.*
- *How you spend your time is a choice.*
- *The choices you make will depend on your values.*
- *Become aware of how you are actually spending your time, and whether or not those efforts are helping you to achieve your goals. If not, you need to change either your goals or the way you spend your time.*
- *Success depends on preparation.*
- *The stress resulting from not planning is greater than the stress of planning.*
- *The one most important key word in staying organized is the word* focus.
- *Understand which goals rank higher in your personal agenda.*
- *Constantly evaluate which of your tasks are truly important and which are merely urgent but not necessarily important.*

4

CREATIVE WAYS TO
SCHEDULE YOUR WORK

Now that we've discussed what you're going to do and how to go about it, it's time to discuss the actual doing of your work. In order to be sure all your activities are carried out, it's imperative that you set aside *specific times* to follow up, so that your projects will get done.

Left-brain people naturally tend to "compartmentalize" their lives—to be methodical, doing one thing at a time—and may get frazzled with too many things happening at once. They prefer to focus exclusively on one aspect of what they are doing, and make plans to do the next step of a project after the preceding step is completed. That won't always work for you if you're a true Arbie, however. You may feel too constricted by working within that framework, since doing things methodically can be about as natural for an Arbie as binding their feet used to be for Chinese women. You can do it, but it doesn't make you comfortable or happy! Arbies can stay structured in the short term, but they find it difficult to sustain their efforts.

Also, you are "simultaneous" if you're an Arbie, meaning you enjoy having more than one thing to do at a time, and are never happier than when you have lots of irons in the fire. It's stimulating, it adds pizzazz to your life. You may enjoy having phones ringing, piles of different types of projects on your desk that need doing, and people stopping by to ask questions all at once.

This variety may be the spice of life to you, because it allows you to switch back and forth quickly from one thing to another without having to concentrate on one specific matter for too long. It makes it difficult to keep single duties scheduled for single times, however, because there is little provision for making sure every aspect of each job gets done.

Scheduling Your Activities

To ensure that a single project gets finished, you need to

- See the whole project.
- Break it down into steps.
- Break those steps down into activities.
- Schedule those activities.

For example, to hire someone to do some decorating (the whole project), you might break it down into these steps:

1. Find the proper person to hire.
2. Discuss your budget, preferences, and needs with your decorator.
3. Choose colors, fabrics, and paints.
4. Set up work and delivery dates.

Each of these major steps could then be broken down into specific activities. Activities in the first step might include the following:

- Call wallpaper and fabric shops for recommendations.
- Contact friends who have had decorating done.
- Select names of decorators from the Yellow Pages.

Making Sure Your Work Gets Done

Nothing else can so quickly remove pressure from your mind as the simple act of writing down your reminders and putting them where you know you can see them at the appropriate time. Remember the saying. "On paper, off your mind." We'll therefore discuss various forms of reminders in order for you to choose what serves your style best.

A calendar or appointment book having separate daily pages with times listed in fifteen-minute increments is the most reliable method of scheduling your time. Wall or desk calendars having little boxes for each day are less effective for the average busy individual today.

It would be perfectly natural for Elbies to make a "to do" list, schedule the activities on a calendar, and/or fill out a standard project sheet (discussed below) for different jobs.

If you now use a wall or desk calendar, it isn't necessary to take a great deal of time to set up a calendar book. Rather, let it happen naturally. Start by taking a few minutes to transfer all of your current appointment dates from your wall calendar to the specific time on the appropriate calendar book page.

From that point on, begin entering not only all of your appointments at the appropriate times, but (and this is very im-

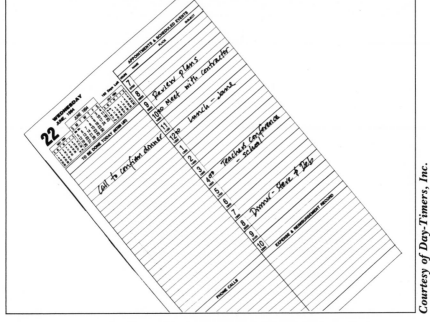

Courtesy of Day-Timers, Inc.

Transfer your appointments from your wall or desk calendar to a book with daily calendar pages.

portant) *begin penciling in reminders of when you intend to do your work, too.*

For example, let's say that on a Monday night you are planning a redecorating project, and are thinking about when you can begin finding the right decorator. You might know that you'll be too busy in the next two days, but think you can get started Thursday afternoon. Therefore, you can block out some time at 1:00 P.M. on Thursday's calendar page to begin making calls.

That Thursday, as you learn of names to call, you are told to call a certain man on Friday because he isn't in today, so you enter that reminder on tomorrow's page, and so forth. Each time you are reminded of another step, enter that at a specific time on your calendar page. Remember to schedule each thing you need to do, and soon that calendar book will become your "bible"—you'll wonder how you ever functioned without it.

Lists, Stick-on Notes, and Project Sheets

No book on organization would be complete without mention of the venerable "list." Everyone makes lists, and we heartily support the idea of writing down reminders of what you need to do.

There are devices other than lists that an Arbie can use to "get organized." Blank cards or "stick-on notes" can be a great help in "getting it all together."

You can set up a "project sheet" for a complex venture. At the top you can list the name of the project, then a short description of what you want to accomplish. Below that, you will want to list the steps it will take to accomplish the enterprise.

There are various ways to go about producing a project sheet. For your decorating project, you can first write each of the foregoing steps and activities on separate cards or stick-on notes in any order, as you think of them, and then arrange them into the order in which you will actually do them. These notes can then be placed in order on your project sheet.

Or you can list them in order by writing on the page itself, and sticking the notes on the appropriate pages of your calendar book, according to the time and day you intend to do them.

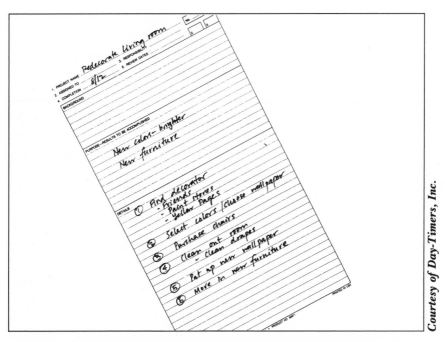

Write down the steps of your project as you think of them, then transfer them in order onto a project sheet.

They can also be placed on a bulletin board or on the wall above your desk, or anywhere else you may want to see them.

A word about putting notes to yourself on walls, bulletin boards, computer terminals, and so on: If you're a normal Arbie, you prefer to keep your reminders out where you can see them, rather than "hiding" them in a calendar book, file, or other obscure place where you're afraid you'll never find them again. This is fine up to a point, but there are drawbacks.

First, the tendency is to put *all* your reminders out in front of you, even though some of those tasks don't actually have to be done until sometime later on. By leaving them out in front of you in the meantime, you're only adding to the confusion of your work space and unintentionally adding to your stress by having constant reminders out in front of you, even though they refer to tasks that don't have to be done now.

Second, one is inclined to keep adding more and more of these little notes, without ever removing any. These can quickly turn into an eyesore, but, worse, pretty soon all those little notes tend to become a blur, and it becomes difficult to focus on just one important one. So it's all right to put up notes as reminders to yourself, but use some precautions:

- Try putting up only those reminders to yourself that are of earth-shaking importance.
- Put up only those notes that you intend to handle today, and keep the rest on future calendar pages, in a file, or someplace else where you can find them.
- Then, *remember to take them down again!*

Remember that every item you leave out in the open creates one more piece of clutter, which results in difficulty in finding things, which results in lost time, which results in frustration. (See Chapter 9.)

If you like to rely on creativity (rather than making a regular "boring" list of things to do), you might experiment with making different types of project sheets, calendars, or "to do" lists.

An alternate way to make a project sheet would be to use a sheet of paper to represent the decorating project. Turn the paper horizontally and draw a line across the middle of the sheet. The left end of the line would illustrate the beginning of the project, the center part would depict the ongoing activities, and the right end of the line would portray the completed project. Then write in the steps to be taken along the way, along with appropriate dates.

For your daily or weekly calendar page, you can also draw a "time line." This can be drawn on a single sheet of paper, on a blackboard, or—if you prefer to do things expansively—even across a six-foot-long banner on the wall! On the left end of the line is the time you get up in the morning; noon is near the center; and whatever time you go to bed is on the right end. Things needing to be done can then be jotted down at appropriate places along the line.

Or, instead of writing in notes at specific times, you can

simply sprinkle stick-on notes across the page or board (keeping in mind the foregoing suggestions).

Another technique particularly enjoyed by Arbies is to draw branches off the time line to indicate main projects, with other lines branching off from those to indicate associated tasks.

Project sheets provide a good, standardized method of tracking steps and activities, but you still need to incorporate those activities into a calendar reminder system, to be sure you establish a time for getting them done.

Mind-Mapping

A variable on the above, and another creative way to put ideas down on paper, is called mind-mapping. This process involves drawing a rough circle in the middle of a sheet of paper to represent a central idea you want to explore. From the edges of this central circle, draw lines out in any direction

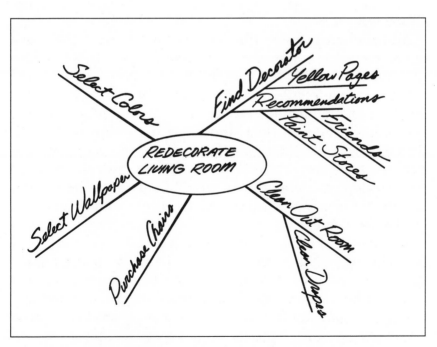

Try the mind-mapping technique for planning a new project.

to indicate related ideas. Subordinate thoughts can be added as branches off those protruding lines.

Mind-mapping can be used to explore ideas for achieving goals, to figure out activities that will be needed to complete a project, to brainstorm various ways to go about doing something, or in any other creative way you may want to utilize it. In the case of the decorating project, "Decorating the living room" could be written in the central circle. Lines emanating from the circle could represent *steps* in the project: "Find decorator to hire"; "How to pay for project"; "Choose colors, fabrics, and paints"; "Schedule work and delivery dates"; and so on. "Activities" lines could then branch out from the "steps" lines. Ideas for choosing a decorator might include "Call wallpaper and fabric shops for recommendations"; "Contact friends who have had decorating done"; "Select and call decorators from the Yellow Pages." These activities can then be scheduled in your calendar book or time line.

Charting Your Year

Arbies often envision the year differently from the traditional, rectangular way years are printed on cards, wall calendars, and checkbook registers (by Elbies, of course).

Some people see their year as a straight line, as in the description of the time line above, with January on the far left, February on the next right, and so forth, continuing through December on the far right. Others envision their year as a circle or a pie-shaped clock, with months shown clockwise or even counterclockwise; that is, with January at twelve o'clock, and the other months proceeding in order around the hours on the clock face.

A "pie" can also represent the hours of a day, or the days of the week. As an Arbie, you may want to create your own unique visual concept of a calendar. Whatever kind of reminder system you create, guard against spending too much time creating the system and too little time putting it to good use. Once again, consider the clutter factor and try to set up your system so that it's eye-pleasing as well as useful. Don't make it overly complicated, because the more difficult it is to use, the less likely you'll be to stick with it. It should be as simple and as natural to use as possible.

Working Your Plans Through to a Conclusion

As we've said, starting a job is the easy part. Following through and then finishing is what's hard—but completion is also what brings about the greatest satisfaction. Some people, however, bring their goals *almost* to a conclusion—but not quite. Perhaps because of fear of success, they will quit just before they finish. Perhaps they are afraid they will be judged and criticized if their completed project is imperfect, so they allow fear of failure to obstruct completion. In fact, these people seem to live by the "ninety-percent rule"—they finish ninety percent of their work ninety percent of the time. This often means that the materials connected with uncompleted tasks are left lying around, rather than being put away.

The next time you set out to do your work, look over what you want to do, and before starting something new, ask yourself what else could be completed instead? *There's no greater feeling than finally putting a completed project behind you!* Like an irritant, the best reason for getting it done once and for all is that you won't have to look at the unfinished job anymore, and in some instances you will be able to swell your chest while you admire the finished product. It's a great ego booster to write a "done" list of all the things you have accomplished at the end of the day.

SUMMARY

- *Be creative in the way you choose to maintain a unique scheme of reminders and calendars for yourself.*
- *As you think of something to do, write it down NOW! (This note to yourself is not a reminder to* do *the work, but a reminder to* put it on your calendar.

- *Schedule your tasks along with your appointments in your calendar.*
- *Break down projects into steps.*
- *Set up a project sheet for complex ventures.*
- *Remember that there's no greater feeling than putting a completed project behind you.*

5

LAUNCHING YOUR VISIONS
INTO ACTION

The first four chapters of this book encouraged you to clarify your organizing style, your dreams, and your priorities; in this chapter we will discuss practical applications of when and how to go about putting your dreams into action.

One definition of the Buddhist term *nirvana* is "any place or condition of great peace or bliss." An Americanized version of nirvana might include having ample time for individual pursuits, without the constant pressure of "having too much to do." This is what good management is all about. It simply means using your time to its best advantage, so you have time left over to pursue your personal interests. By using the time-management tips in this book, you can get your work out of the way and have more free time to do what you want.

Convergent Thinking

When Elbies consider what needs to be done, they have little trouble prioritizing, because the left brain tends toward "convergent thinking." That is, it's very good at looking at any number of seemingly unrelated items and bringing them together. For example, a doctor must utilize left-brain convergent thinking to diagnose an illness. She needs to analyze a multitude of her patient's symptoms and deduce the specific cause of those symptoms. In the same way, most Elbies can fairly easily consider the various tasks needing to be done and choose the most important thing to do first.

Divergent Thinking

The right brain works in exactly the opposite way. When an Arbie ponders how to use time, innumerable ideas pop up all at once. This is a result of the inherent right-brain characteristic of "divergent thinking." *Divergent* means branching out, from one to many. That's why right-brain people are very good at brainstorming.

When Arbies try to decide on the best use of their time, they will be drawn simultaneously in any number of directions. Such a simple question as "What shall I do next?" can set off a veritable explosion of ideas in the Arbie's head. To complicate matters further, each of those ideas produces yet another thought, leading off in still another direction.

Harnessing that kind of mental energy is, of course, the challenge for anyone possessing this incredible talent. (It's too bad that Elbies have long used the derogatory term "scatter-brained" to refer to people who have this talent, rather than giving them appropriate credit for their unique abilities.)

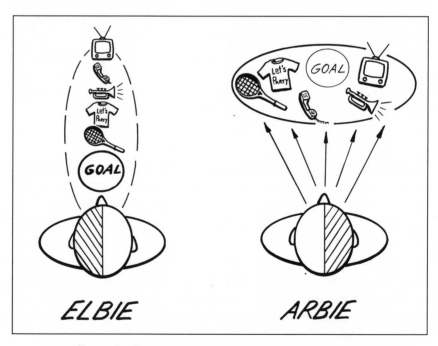

An Elbie's thinking is convergent; an Arbie's is divergent.

Since the right brain is also nonlinear, it alone cannot put work into methodical order. As a result, Arbies tend to grab first this file, then that paper, hoping—knowing, rather—that everything will eventually fall into place. In the meantime, however, this seemingly impractical flailing about will bring Elbie associates to their knees, crying in desperation, "Why, oh, why can't you just do things in order?"

Lakein's Questions

In his book *How to Get Control of Your Time and Your Life,* Alan Lakein asks "Lakein's Questions": (1) "What is the best use of my time now?" (2) "Am I wasting my time?" and (3) "Is there a way to simplify this task?" These three questions are of utmost importance in managing your time.

"What Is the Best Use of My Time Now?" Ask yourself this first question several times every day. Start during your planning sessions, asking yourself what would be the best (i.e., the most productive) way to spend each hour of your day. Then, during your day, ask yourself that same question at each turning point—when you finish each task, when you are puzzled about how to go about doing something, or when someone makes a spontaneous suggestion about doing something. A suggestion such as "Let's run down to the company library and research that point" may or may not be a good use of your time now. Will it help you to achieve your current goals—or will it be sidetracking you from your main focus? You need to think convergently—that is, taking all of the current issues and bringing them down to a single decision—about what the best use of your time would be now.

"Am I Wasting My Time?" "Is There a Way to Simplify This Task?" Lakein's second and third questions are also important.

Arbies can become so totally immersed in what they are doing that they aren't concerned about getting to the point of their task in the most direct way. It's the *doing* of the project that absorbs their interest; they are more concerned with the process than with the product.

It's ironic that many people spend an excessive amount of time preparing to get organized. Rather than spending appropriate time doing their planning, and then pitching in and getting the job done, these people can sometimes waste vast amounts of time, taking up their whole working period in just getting organized. "Over-organizers" may set up intricate and complex plans to get themselves organized, find that those plans don't work, spend further time setting up something else—and on and on.

The Global Approach

Another trait that detracts from Arbies' ability to focus on a single job is their holistic approach. The right brain doesn't see individual trees, it sees the whole forest. Arbies are therefore constantly aware of the global aspect of a whole project, even while they are working on a single piece. (Left-brain readers who find this strange have only to remember the reverse situation: how they are nearly always aware of time, while Arbies may be oblivious to it.)

To comprehend this global approach, imagine running a video camera. Arbies would tend to focus the lens at a wide angle so they could view the whole scene. In fact, they may need to see the complete picture as a first step in order to put things into a meaningful context. You may recognize this instinct while shopping for clothes. If you're an Arbie, you may want to look at all the racks of clothes in the store before beginning to whittle down your choices.

Because the right brain sees the whole rather than specifics, it's difficult for the Arbie to break down work into parts. Knowing when to switch from the global aspect to the specific parts of a job is a recurring problem. For example, when a desk needs cleaning off, an Arbie may immediately become overwhelmed by seeing the whole desk and its clutter as a single unit; it will be hard to figure out where to begin. Such people may start by randomly picking up papers in one place and putting them down in another, rearranging all the piles but not putting anything away. Then they might become engrossed in reading a fascinating magazine article they found in one of the piles. (Sound familiar?)

Because of these traits, Arbies end up doing work the hard

way instead of the easy way—at least according to judgmental left-brainers—and receive the brunt of Elbies' criticism and complaints. Without tenacious self-esteem, these right-brain dominants may even begin to feel guilt and shame. (This subject is discussed in Chapter 13.)

If you tend toward the global approach, you need to learn how to zoom in your video lens and focus on one particular aspect of a project at a time. You may have to imagine putting on blinders so that you can focus on single objects rather than on the whole picture.

In the end, however, when you do complete a task, even though you may have gone about it in an unconventional manner, remember that your work may end up being of much superior quality to that of your Elbie counterparts.

"Do It Now" Versus "Note It Now and Do It Later"

Someone has said, "The organized person is someone who has already done what you are thinking of doing"; in general, we agree. Most highly organized people will tell you that one of their secrets is to "do it now." This works well for them, and we recommend it highly—with some clarification.

It's a simple fact that most highly organized people are already caught up on their work; they aren't surrounded by piles of clutter awaiting attention. They're on schedule with their projects, and they have time and confidence to deal with unexpected events. Therefore, when they see something that needs to be done, they can simply take care of it right then. They get it out of the way and don't have to worry about it anymore.

If you're an Arbie, on the other hand, your work style may be just the opposite. You may be hurrying to meet deadlines. Trying to catch up on other projects, you have piles of clutter awaiting your attention; everywhere you look, you see things that need to be done. Trying to "do it now" every time a new task comes up will drive you stark raving mad. If you try, you're liable to start one thing, then be confronted with a second, and soon you'll have created even greater disorder, your time will be gone, and you'll feel even more behind the eight-ball because you will have accomplished very little.

Mr. Jones, one of our clients and a "do-it-now'er to a fault," by his own definition, provided an excellent example of this.

One Saturday, as he and his family were cleaning out their garage, Mr. Jones began finding things that needed to be done. The lawnmower blade needed sharpening, so he stopped cleaning and removed the blade to take it in for grinding; a nylon rope end needed repair, so he rebraided and melted the end so that it would remain intact, and so forth.

After he had already been sidetracked from his cleaning innumerable times, he came across the rudder from their little sailboat, and saw that it needed revarnishing. When he headed for the car to drive to the hardware store to buy varnish, his wife lost patience. "Here's a pad and pencil," she said. "From now until we finish cleaning, when you find something that needs doing, write it down so you won't forget. After we're done, you can work from that list and spend the rest of the day making repairs." They were then able to complete the cleaning in short order.

Here's a guide to help you decide whether you should "do it now" or "note it now and schedule it for later":

Do It Now if . . .
- *it's an emergency*
- *it finishes your present task*
- *it can be done quickly and will not interrupt or distract from your present schedule*

Note It Now and Schedule It for Later if . . .
- *it's not an emergency*
- *it will interrupt what you are doing now*

Most Productive Versus Least Productive Time Frames

Sometimes the time isn't right to work on a high-priority job. Perhaps the beginning of your day is very noisy, with lots of interruptions, and you need quiet concentration to focus on your work. Therefore, it's only necessary to *schedule* your high-priority work first. As long as you're secure in the knowledge that it will get done at a certain time, it may be more effective to delay doing it until an appropriate time.

Along these same lines, sometimes it's best to work on your toughest job first, whether it's cleaning the basement or writing your resumé, even if it's not your highest priority. If you delay a dreaded job, it will only weigh on you all day (or week or month), and you'll end up doing it when you're already tired and frustrated—the worst time to do anything difficult.

Choose the Best Task and Do It at the Best Time

After selecting the most productive task, do it at a time when you can accomplish it most effectively. Perform difficult tasks (either physically demanding jobs or those mental tasks that are hardest for you) at your peak energy times. This includes making tough decisions. Do work you enjoy most (even if it's physically strenuous) at low-ebb times. Don't try to do difficult work against all odds—such as when you know you'll have lots of interruptions.

Instant Success

The concept of instant success can be helpful toward deciding how fruitfully you are spending your time and your life. Instant success means being successful *at this moment.* Five minutes ago or ten minutes from now don't matter—what's important is *right now,* this instant. If you are actively involved in doing something you *value* (even if it isn't much fun), then you are being successful in this instant—you are enjoying instant success.

This may mean doing calculations that you hate, but that are involved in starting a business you're excited about; it may mean spending quality time with your child, even though important work awaits your attention; or it might mean taking badly needed time for yourself. Good time management—being successful—doesn't necessarily mean working hard or doing something difficult for you; it means doing activities you regard as important to achieving what you want in life.

Instant success is easier to achieve, of course, when it involves an agreeable activity. It takes real motivation, however, to be consistently instantly successful at non-fun jobs. (How to get yourself to tackle difficult work will be discussed in various other parts of this book.)

EXERCISE: "FIVE MINUTES BEFORE THE HOUR"

If you have a desk or other surface that is cluttered, set aside five minutes before each hour to clear off one small part of it. At the end of your five-minute session, set a timer for fifty-five minutes so you'll remember the next five-minute period.

What can you get done in only five minutes? Try it—you'll be surprised. At the end of two weeks you'll see a vast improvement. This example of Instant Success will bring a feeling of genuine satisfaction. There will be much more about clutter control in Chapter 8.

Learn How Long Tasks Take

There's a great deal of wisdom in the old saying, "Time flies when you're having fun." People naturally tend to overestimate the time it takes to do the things they dislike, and underestimate the time it takes to do the things they enjoy. A person who likes computer programming, for instance, can sit practically without moving at a terminal for whole days, yet complain about how long a one-hour church service lasts, or even about how long it takes to get out of the parking lot after a service. Activities like talking to someone you enjoy, reading, or working on a favorite hobby can easily take more time than you originally estimate.

Because of the practical, logical capability of the left brain, Elbies are more often realistic about how long tasks take (although they still make excuses that they "don't have time" to do things they don't want to do, just as Arbies do). Arbies, however, tend to be unrealistic about how long it will take them to accomplish their tasks. They will actually be more prone to *believe* they don't have time to do certain things—to clean up after themselves, for instance. For this reason, it's helpful to figure out how long it really takes you to accomplish your tasks.

Betty, one of our clients, was consistently late for work until she timed how long it took to apply her cosmetics. After finding it took twice as long as she thought, she started getting ready earlier and then began getting along better with her supervisor, because she was nearly always on time.

Another client, Jeff, remembered that one day he was in a hurry to get out the door to an appointment, when he became aware of what he was telling himself: that he didn't have time to replace the files lying on his desk. Forcing himself to return, he counted off the seconds as he replaced the folders in the drawer. He realized for the first time that it took him less than four seconds to replace those folders—an infinitesimal delay—and being in such a hurry that he couldn't leave a few seconds later was not a sufficient reason for not replacing things.

Since one's imagination is usually greater than one's physical ability, add at least twenty-five percent more time than you estimate it will take you to accomplish your work. If you think it will take forty-five minutes to write a business letter, you'll do well to add an extra fifteen minutes, and give yourself a full hour. By allowing for interruptions, you won't constantly feel you are running behind on your time schedule.

Add zest to your life by buying a timer and experimenting with how long it takes to accomplish what you have to do. Or turn on the radio and get your filing done before the news comes on at half past the hour. Finish your telephoning before your coffee break; have your lawn mowed before the football game begins. You'll enjoy a sense of accomplishment and then be able to relax. Making a game out of getting your work done is great motivation.

DIVIDE YOUR WORK INTO YOUR TIME

Try dividing your work into your time, an especially good technique for Arbies. If you have two hours to clean house, divide the number of rooms into your time. If you have six rooms to clean, divide those two hours (120 minutes) by six. You'll have twenty minutes to clean each room. Make a game of it.

2 hours = 120 minutes

120 minutes ÷ 6 rooms = 20 minutes per room

This same concept can be translated into cleaning out desk drawers, making a series of phone calls, doing appraisals, or drawing charts. Though each part may not demand equal time, you can first break the segments down to an average, then allow more time for certain facets, while shortening the time allocated for others. This encourages you to get your work done in an allotted amount of time, and then to move on to your next chore. Use your imagination to add some amusement to this process (but don't make it so elaborate that it overshadows the work to be done).

Fill Your Time with One Job

It's helpful to decide how much time you have to work, and choose a task that will fit into that slot of time. If you have a whole afternoon to work, you can fill it with a thousand little tasks, and then perhaps wonder at the end of the day what you did with your time. You know you were busy, but what do you have to show for it?

If you have half a day, ask yourself what half-day projects need doing. Even though you may dread it, do you need to write an account analysis? Could you paint a room? Do you need to make a series of deliveries that will take several hours? Apply this technique of choosing the largest job to fill the time available in one week, one day, or one hour.

If you're an Arbie who is happiest with several things going at once, you can apply the same rule in a slightly different way. If you have four hours, choose two to four tasks that, when added together, will take a total of four hours. This will allow you to maintain your interest without overburdening your schedule. Conversely, fill short time slots with small tasks. Don't start a long, involved project when you have only fifteen minutes to work. Ask yourself what fifteen-minute task needs to be done.

Even tiny amounts of time, such as thirty seconds or two minutes, hold opportunities for accomplishment. Most people never realize how long forty-five seconds can seem until they have waited in front of a microwave oven counting, "Forty-five, forty-four, forty-three, forty-two . . ." You can clear a couple of things off a counter in that time, wipe up a spill, or throw away some trash.

Utilize the Best Times to Do Your Work

Most people are "day people"; that is, they are happy working within the confines of the workaday world, arising at a routine time each morning, working a daytime shift, and going to bed at about the same time each night. Within that broad framework, people have vastly differing peaks and valleys of energy and lethargy. One person arises bright and alert, goes strong until late morning, and then tends to wilt until later in the day. Another starts slowly, gradually builds energy, and does his or her best work around noon. And then there are night people. They, of course, may be most alert and have the most energy beginning around ten o'clock at night, and they may last until three o'clock in the morning.

We know of no actual correlation that has been made between right- and left-brain dominance and day or night people. However, we want to compare them here simply because Arbies and night people both tend to be "out of sync" with the rest of the world. Being out of sync doesn't mean being wrong—or right, for that matter—but merely different. Whatever your rhythm is, you'll do well to live by it to the extent possible. For instance, if you're a night person and can obtain swing-shift work, sign up for that shift.

The important aspect of knowing your biological rhythms is to become aware of your unique daily peaks and valleys of energy so that you can do your most difficult work during peak times and your easiest work during your valleys. Keep in mind that the word *difficult* doesn't necessarily refer to heavy physical activities or hard work in the general sense. What you consider hard or easy may be entirely different for the person next to you. If writing letters is easy for you, then write them during low-energy times; if it is difficult for you, however, write during peak energy times.

Decision-making is especially difficult during low-energy times. The time to pick out wallpaper is not when you're tired and drained. You want to make that decision when you're fresh and thinking clearly. If you're an Arbie, you'll do well to give extra consideration to this concept. If you're prone to act impulsively, you may make decisions that aren't in your best interest when you're tired or out of sorts, rather than being practical and waiting until a better time.

Messages Versus Chitchat

For centuries people have known that certain injuries to the left hemisphere of the brain affected the victim's speech; thus it was no surprise when modern researchers confirmed that language ability resides in the left brain. Combining language with analytical thinking and other left-brain traits, Elbies find it easy to be articulate. People who "put their left brain in gear" can say specifically what they mean, get to the point, and move on.

Arbies have several attributes that affect their speech patterns. For them, talking takes on special meaning. Recent research indicates that feelings are processed by the right brain. (Other parts of the brain, including the pre-frontal lobes and limbic system, are also involved in emotions.) Therefore, Arbies tend to be more people-oriented; they truly care about others, and are naturally attuned to feelings and emotions and tend to be intuitive about others' up and downs.

Since humor, another right-brain attribute, is most enjoyed when shared with other people, these tendencies often combine to make Arbies especially friendly, chatty, warm, fun-loving people who enjoy talking. These wonderful traits, however, can also be a curse. In the same way that their environments tend to accumulate clutter, so can their conversations. Because of the divergent thinking described earlier, some Arbies tend to ramble in their conversations and have difficulty getting to the point of a story. They don't always know how to express what they want to say. Or, fearful of hurting someone's feelings, they may have trouble bringing a conversation to a conclusion. At other times they may know what they are talking about and expect that the person to whom they are speaking will understand, when in fact they haven't actually verbalized the point they are making.

Cluttered speech can be a true handicap in the business world. Busy corporate left-brain dominants want to get to the point as quickly as possible. They don't want long-drawn-out explanations about how much work it took to do research, how bad someone made you feel, or even, sadly, how things are in your personal life. This is not to say there aren't many appropriate times for prolonged friendly chats, but we're referring to those times when the pressure is on to get work done.

Be sensitive, then, to how you use other people's time. One valuable rule in business discussions is to keep your discourse focused on what your listeners want and need to hear, and what they will be able to understand, rather than on what you know or feel like talking about. That helps keep you to the point and not waste others' time.

Try to avoid unnecessary details such as "I got out of bed, put on my robe and slippers, brushed my teeth," and so on; the other person understands you did all that without your saying it. Your story can be more effective and you'll be more interesting without such details.

Also, whether you're an Arbie or not, remember, when you hear other people repeating long lists of what they've been doing, that they may be experiencing stress and looking for approval of their efforts. Whether it's a homemaker who recites a long list of errands, a student who complains about all his or her homework, or a salesman who lists the trials and tribulations of closing a deal, try to realize that these people are not so much complaining as seeking a pat on the back for their dogged efforts. When you recognize this phenomenon, it's all right to interrupt and say, "It sounds as if you really worked hard." This will work magic in making the other person feel appreciated, and will save you from having to listen to the rest of the boring details.

If you're the offending party who offers more details than others want to hear, you can increase your chances for empathy by condensing your message into something like "I'm really tired from running errands for three hours in heavy traffic this afternoon." This saves everyone time, too.

Delegation

Arbies are very good at creating projects. They can come up with beautiful, colorful, energetic plans of great complexity. Because they tend to be creative, a single pinecone can inspire them to undertake a whole new elaborate decorative project. Arbies are good at starting these projects, but, alas! because the right brain needs constant stimulation, their interest in a single line of thought soon wanes, and the original inspiration is lost as time passes. The consequence may be another project added to an already long list of ventures begun but not brought to fruition.

When you come up with a unique concept, it's natural to

think, "I'm the only one who can do this right." As an Arbie who has creative ideas, you need to recognize that most jobs require left-brain activities to complete them. In other words, you may need to let go and find someone else to handle certain aspects of your project.

Of course, letting someone else do your routine chores is one thing, but handing over your pet project may be another matter. Delegation, however, is a skill that must be mastered by anyone who wants to use his or her time effectively. If you know instinctively that someone else can handle one aspect of your project better than you can, remind yourself that this will free you to do other, more creative work.

Another delegation hurdle is expressed in the idea, "I hate to ask someone else to do this tedious thing for me." But remember that what may be tedious for you may be quite enjoyable for a different type of person.

There are multitudes of ways to delegate. For instance, one female business owner was criticized by acquaintances for hiring a driver while she "sat in the backseat and gabbed on the phone." She knows, however, that almost anyone can drive, but she made good use of her time by doing work that she, and only she, could do as a business owner. The moral of the story is *Do what you do best, and delegate to others what they can do just as well as you can.*

Another way to delegate is to trade jobs with someone else. If you aren't in a position to delegate downward, don't overlook your peers. All of us have some chores we like and others we dislike, but these will vary from one person to the next. One woman may not mind ironing, but misses the freedom of shopping without children, while her next-door neighbor loves little children but intensely dislikes ironing. Or an office worker may dislike setting up a color-coded filing system but enjoy filling out certain reports, while his co-worker may have the opposite likes and dislikes. These are prime possibilities for trading jobs. Think of ways to delegate or trade jobs that you don't like or that you don't do well naturally.

Third, try delegating by hiring a professional and learning from him or her. That way, the next time you can handle the same job more easily yourself. Professionals know which efforts produce the greatest yield. It's sometimes said that "amateurs work hard; professionals work smart." Besides their expertise, most professionals are proud of their knowledge and feel complimented when you ask them to explain how they do their work so well.

Our friend Jane was having difficulty landscaping a strategic spot near her front driveway. After spending many hours without achieving satisfying results, she finally hired a professional landscaper to do the job. She was amazed when he and his helper did a nearly perfect job on the area in just forty-five minutes. But she observed their techniques carefully, and learned to streamline her own garden skills in the process.

On her consulting jobs, one of the authors of this book has gotten innumerable clients started setting up filing systems, and then been able to leave at a midway point because the clients got the gist of how to go about it and were easily able to complete the job themselves.

Consider Alternatives

This is a technique Arbies would do well to specialize in: When you must do an unwelcome task, consider more agreeable alternative ways to approach it. Because of their structured tendencies, Elbies may have trouble with this, but if you're an Arbie, this is your chance to let your creative abilities run free. If an errand entails a particularly hectic drive involving busy freeways, harrowing left turns, or a threatening neighborhood, be creative! Think of ways to leave earlier, take a different route, or combine the errand with a pleasant side trip.

To reduce the burden of big chores, recruit groups of people to work with you—provide snacks and beverages for a house-painting "party," or add color to drab jobs in other ways: dress up in ridiculous garb to work with children; listen to wild music to give you energy. Being as creative as possible can help you reduce the dread factor.

Utilize the Trash Can

Finally, the best time-saving tip of all is to use your "personal organization box"—your wastebasket—regularly. Since Arbies are often savers (this trait will be discussed in Chapter 8), they don't tend to toss things away readily. For now, we only want to say that the fewer items you have, the less time it will take you to manage them. Utilize your wastebasket liberally.

SUMMARY

- *Use good time management to*
    1. *relieve the pressure of tight time constraints*
    2. *lift the feeling of being burdened by having too much to do*
    3. *give you leisure time to pursue your own interests*
- *Decide what to do first, since divergent thinking produces multiple possibilities.*
- *To avoid bouncing from one activity to another, choose the best time for a given activity.*
- *Concentrate on one aspect of a project at a time.*
- *Make a realistic estimate of how long each task will take. (It may not take as long as you imagine.)*
- *Budget your time as carefully as you budget your money; use long slots of time for large activities, short periods for small jobs.*
- *Do difficult work during peak energy times.*
- *In conversation, save your best stories for appropriate times and people who are best equipped to appreciate them.*
- *Learn to let go and allow other people to contribute their skills to certain aspects of work they can do better than you, so that everyone's time and talents can be used most effectively.*
- *Create ways to liven up dull, routine tasks.*

6

THE ODD COUPLE WITHIN US

Excuses

Procrastination means to put off or defer action, to delay or habitually postpone. The question is, when does purposely delaying low-priority work become procrastination?

The answer varies with each individual. You must ask yourself, "Am I making excuses, or am I making a sincere, conscious decision?" "I don't have time" is an excuse; "That isn't the best use of my time now" represents a conscious decision.

Everyone makes excuses sometimes. When we don't accomplish something we intended to accomplish, or are delaying doing what we don't want to do, we tend to excuse ourselves by saying things like "I'm too busy," "I'm too tired," "I'll do it later," "I didn't have time," or "Creative people are messy." Let's explore some of these excuses more closely.

"I'm Too Busy, or "I Don't Have Time"

When we say we don't have enough time to do certain things, it is not, in fact, true. What we may be really saying is that we are using our overactivity as a rationalization for not doing the things we didn't want to do in the first place. Our unspoken alibi is "I'm keeping myself so busy that I will be able to avoid doing what I really don't want to do, so I won't feel guilty about not doing it."

When you say, "I don't have the time to clean my desk every day," think about this: If someone were to give you a thousand dollars every single day you cleared off your desk, would you find time to do it? (We all would!)

"I don't have time" is probably the world's greatest cop-out. When we say we don't have time, what we are really saying is "I choose not to spend my time in that way." The latter statement is not an excuse, but denotes a conscious choice on our part. We *chose* to do something else that we considered more important. The question then becomes "Were the other things you did instead really more important, or did you merely do those other things in order to get out of what you didn't want to do?"

Let's say you "didn't have time" to balance your checkbook one Saturday, but slept late in the morning, went shopping in the afternoon, and attended a party that night. It may be that you had been working very long hours and were physically and emotionally in need of a break from your hard work. If this is true, then your statement needs to be "I needed some down-time and chose not to balance my checkbook Saturday," rather than making the excuse that you "didn't have time." This helps crystallize your thinking and puts your life in perspective.

When we make excuses, we are deceiving ourselves. Even though we may be totally honest people who would never lie to anyone else, we may not be aware that we are being dishonest with ourselves.

"Creative People Are Messy"

This is a legendary excuse, usually accompanied by a chuckle and an impish smile. There is often an implied conviction that it's "cute" to be messy—that the perpetrator loves being spontaneous and that it's "more fun" to just leave things as they are and go off and do something else more exciting.

Two Reasons to Do Your Work

Only you can decide whether you are procrastinating or making conscious decisions, but here are some guidelines that may help you. Try asking yourself these simple questions:

1. **Is it high priority?** ("Will doing this particular task help me to achieve my goals?") Obviously, you first need to know which dream you want to accomplish to answer this question.

Getting yourself to ask the question in the first place can be difficult because, unless you put your left brain into gear, you will tend to be completely absorbed in the here and now. If you are visually oriented, you will be inclined to become easily distracted and then preoccupied with whatever is in view—an interesting article in a magazine, for instance—rather than thinking, "What is the best use of my time now?"

If your goals include getting a promotion, becoming better educated, keeping your desk in order so you can find things, or maintaining good personal relationships, which of those is most important to you? As demonstrated in Chapter 1, it's up to you to decide what is or is not important in your life, and to focus on work that will help you achieve your highest priorities. This requires sifting out what is unimportant and saying no to those lower-priority, less productive pastimes. But remember that such things as cleaning off your desk cannot be avoided too long, because they will quickly inhibit your ability to achieve your higher plans.

2. Is it an irritant? The second reason to do something or get rid of a "to do" is that it becomes an irritant. Many times, low-priority items are left to stack up. These tasks still need to be done, but since they are not high priority, they continue to be delayed. Arbies often keep visual reminders for an inordinate length of time. Such reminders nag their owners daily, yet nothing is done about the jobs they represent. These, then, become irritants.

Author Stephanie Winston first brought irritants to our attention in her book *Getting Organized.* It was an eye-opener for us then, and we have since come to appreciate the importance of this seemingly mundane phenomenon.

> Our client George, a hospital director, knew all year long he had to make an annual report to his board. Past experience had taught him that he should be collecting information throughout the year and compiling it as he went along, to avoid once again burning the midnight oil the night before the meeting and then showing up tired and stressed. Therefore, when appropriate data

showed up he would stack it on his windowsill, so he could see it and remember to work on it.

Sure enough, he never "had time" to work on the report all year long, but it quickly became an irritant because every time he saw that pile he would remind himself, "I've got to start on that report." The potential report was only one of many tasks he kept out because he feared that if he put them away, he would forget to do them.

What George didn't understand was how irritants affected his life—and how they could multiply! He did know, of course, that when he looked at the windowsill on any given day, he was reminded of something to be done. He didn't realize, though, that if he saw that stack of papers just five times in one day, it produced five mental jabs, not just one. (*Bam!* "I've got to get that done." *Bam!* "I've got to get at that report." *Bam!* . . .)

Now if George had only six irritants on his desk (or perhaps stick-on note reminders on his wall or computer terminal), which he saw five times each in a given day, he was receiving not one, not six, but *thirty* reminders of things to be done that day alone. Now *that's* overwhelming—especially when you consider that George was busy doing still other things and had no intention of actually getting to any of those bedeviling irritants that day!

Your Response to Irritants

You can tell whether or not you are "suffering" from irritants by becoming aware of your physical or emotional reaction to them. If you have a lot of clutter and you are perfectly content with "stuff" lying around, then for you the clutter does not constitute an irritant. However, if certain muscles suddenly knot up in your back or neck when you see one of these "to do's," or if you develop a headache or stomachache, you know you have an irritant on your hands.

Perhaps your reaction is more emotional; maybe you suddenly get into a bad mood without a good explanation, and feel as though you're carrying the weight of the world on your back or as if you've been covered by a black cloud or a wet blanket. Each person develops his or her own reaction to irritants, and will nearly always react consistently in his or her own unique manner. By first identifying your reaction, then recognizing the irritant, you can understand how irritants kill contentment. The best reason to get rid of an irritant is to *want it off your mind and out of your life!*

Ironically, the average irritant takes only a few minutes to handle. In most cases you can either do the irritating task (e.g., return a borrowed item or repair something) or simply discard it so you'll never have to look at it again (dispose of a stack of unread magazines, or discard a project started long ago but never finished.)

If you target *just ten minutes per day to get rid of irritants,* you'll be amazed how quickly your mind will begin to feel less cluttered. Once handled, those pesky jobs will quit nagging you, you'll notice how much less you have to do, and you'll be able to relax and focus on more important things in your life.

The Domino Effect

Not only do irritants multiply, they also tend to inhibit productivity. In fact, one of "Murphy's Laws" states, "Regardless of what needs doing, something else must be done first." This is called the "domino effect."

All too often, people are kept from doing larger tasks by a simple little irritant. For instance, our friend Carol was anxious to lay carpeting in two rooms of her house. She knew exactly what carpet she was going to put down and where to get it, and she had the money to buy it. Why didn't she go ahead with the project? Because she wanted to get those two rooms painted first, so her new carpet wouldn't be splattered with paint in the process. She knew what she wanted and could afford it, so why didn't she get the painting done? Because her windows needed puttying first. Why hadn't she gotten the puttying done? Because she didn't know how to do it, nor did she know whom to call to have it done. And so the irritant was inhibiting her productivity. It became a "domino effect."

Brent serves as another example of that same phenomenon. He would arrive at his office without a day's plan in mind and begin digging through a stack of papers on his desk. But as he went through them he would realize that he didn't have the necessary data to act on any of them, so he'd shuffle through the papers, moving them into a new stack one at a time. This would take a good deal of time (and emotional energy) without accomplishing anything.

In George's case, he promised himself that as soon as he set up a system to prepare his annual report, he would reward himself by taking some seminars about new hospital administrative practices, something that would enhance his abilities considerably. Since he didn't get to the report, however, his education was delayed a full year.

This domino effect is a common malady. How many A.B.D.'s (All But Dissertation) could get their Ph.D.'s and be promoted or receive raises on their jobs, for instance, if only they had finished their dissertation after all those years of graduate study? How many people would entertain more if their homes were neater, cleaner, or redecorated? How many people delay getting pieces of furniture re-covered because they don't know a good upholsterer? That type of list would be unending.

When you have reached the point in your life when everything you try to do is predicated on the accomplishment of something else, *you know your life is out of control.* Something can be done to change it, however, and planning ahead is the key.

The "Odd Couple" Within

Why is it that we delay our work, often in a great show of being "busy"? Why is it that one person may be very good at doing certain types of work, while letting similar jobs go?

The reasons, of course, are many and widely varied—from being right- or left-brain dominant to anxieties learned during childhood, from attitudes formed over a lifetime to depression brought on by current events. These and other factors will be discussed in this chapter to give you better insights into any roadblocks you may be experiencing that are holding you back from accomplishing what you want.

First, it's important to understand that there's a little bit of the "Odd Couple" within every person. One mother with three children, two cats, and a dog proclaimed that "I keep my floors so clean you could eat off them at any time! Unfortunately, you can never eat off my kitchen *table* because it's always piled high with papers."

Another woman admitted that the only thing she hated to do more than ironing was addressing Christmas cards; when she realized this, she finally understood why December was the only month when her ironing got caught up!

The Working-Hard-to-Get-Out-of-Work Syndrome

Some people use every conceivable excuse to avoid working on tasks they dislike. We have dubbed this the Working-Hard-to-Get-Out-of-Work Syndrome, and it can be expressed in the following rule:

> *When a disliked task needs to be done,*
> *any more enjoyable activity ranks a higher priority.*

Perhaps you sometimes find yourself manufacturing almost anything else that seems important at that moment, in order to avoid doing what you don't want to do.

People tend to work on things that are easier for them. Whether it's at the office or at home, you are naturally more comfortable working on things that take the least thought, energy, and decision-making. You want to work on things you already know how to do—things you can do almost automatically. It's easier and more comfortable to work with your current word-processing system, for instance, even though more up-to-date software might improve your efficiency. Or the task may not be easier, but instead may represent a more interesting challenge.

Predictably, an Arbie will tend to fall back into right-brain activities to avoid left-brain work, while the exact opposite is true of an Elbie. For instance, an Arbie might prefer to create a transparency for a speech to avoid cleaning out a desk, while his or her Elbie associate might prefer to clean out the desk to avoid creating a graphic.

Other reasons for allowing routine work to preempt more important tasks is that you perceive your routine tasks to be of a higher priority than the work you are delaying, and you know you will be successful in doing them. Typing letters on your old computer program today would probably seem more important than taking the time to go out to shop for, install, and learn a new software program. (This is, of course, another example of "urgent versus important.")

Even Elbies have a difficult time weighing what is or is not high priority, so, with their analytical and goal-setting abilities in abeyance, it's not surprising that some Arbies find it almost impossible.

BUSYWORK

Deciding what *not* to do is almost more important than deciding what to do. If you try to do everything—just because it has come to your attention—then you aren't thinking objectively enough. The very first consideration to give to *any* work is not *when* it should be done, but rather *whether* it should be done at all. Ask yourself, Is it productive work or busywork?

Busywork takes up time but accomplishes little toward your goals. It is different from recreation or entertainment only in the fact that with busywork you feel busy while engaged in this activity, rather than realizing you are taking time from productive work.

It's one thing to say to yourself consciously, "I'm tired and I'm going to allow myself fifteen minutes to just play with the graphics on my computer." Or, "I deserve some time off, so I'm going to get a cup of coffee and stop by and see so-and-so to chat for a few minutes." These are right-brain recreational interludes that are necessary to alleviate left-brain overload. Those same activities become busywork when you do not consciously intend to take time off but instead use them to get out of doing something else you don't want to do. If you don't stay focused on high-priority work, then you'll automatically spend time on busywork.

Busywork Characteristics

Besides lack of productivity, what are some other ways to distinguish between busywork and "real work?"

1. It has a low priority. Obviously, busywork has a very low priority—so low, in fact, that you can ask yourself, "Will I even remember I did this?" Now, if the activity is eating, sleeping, or taking care of your children, for instance, the answer will be "Yes, I will remember it"—because you'd remember if you didn't eat (you'll get hungry) or didn't sleep (you'll get tired) or if you failed to care for your children (because all sorts of terrible things could potentially happen).

But if you realize, after thinking about what you're doing, that *not doing it* will make no difference in the whole scheme of things, then it's low priority.

2. It is enjoyable. While all "real work" is not necessarily unpleasant, just about all busywork is enjoyable—at least more enjoyable than the alternative. While it may actually be dull or boring, it's still less taxing than something else that needs to be done. If you tend to become engrossed easily in what you're doing, you may end up wasting long periods of time with non-productive busywork.

3. It can be used as a distancing tool. Too often—sad, but true—people engage in activities to give the appearance of being busy in order to avoid close relationships. The infamous workaholic would fall into this category, creating work to be done to avoid the discomfort of intimacy—usually with a spouse or children—but this could be avoidance of perceived "superiors" or others as well.

4. It can be perfectionistic. As in the preceding point, expending an inappropriate amount of energy can also be a symptom of busywork, but all busywork doesn't necessarily involve perfectionism. You can see, however, that spending longer than necessary on any given task would constitute busywork.

Busywork and the Arbie

One reason the Arbie is hard-pressed to focus on left-brain productive work is his or her unwillingness to *give up* the limitless choices of ways to spend time. As an Arbie, if you can't stop to daydream or to read an article of interest or to pass your time any way you like, you may experience a sense of loss.

Accepting limitations takes on a totally different meaning for the Arbie than it has for the Elbie. In fact, placing limitations on an Arbie might be compared to removing structure from the life of an Elbie—like saying, "Okay, from now on there will be no set times for anything—no rules to follow, no reason to depend on anyone for anything." The Elbie would be likely to freak out.

Removing structure from a left-brain-dominant person would be like setting that person out alone on a raft in the middle of a large lake, without oars. He or she would be completely adrift, without direction or destination. (Ironically, were it not for the physical danger, the Arbie side would probably love such an adventure, watching with wonder where the winds and waves would take him or her.)

In the same way that the Elbie needs structure, the Arbie needs freedom of choice. If you're an Arbie, you can solve this dilemma by working on structured types of work for only short periods of time, setting aside periods for constructive right-brain activities intermittently. This will relieve the tedium induced by left-brain activities. You could write checks for a while, for instance, and then stop and do some pleasant but necessary telephoning, then return to check-writing, and so on. By consciously designing some right-brain relief from "drudgery," the structured activities can be accomplished without undue stress.

Saying No
Many, many people are unable to say no. Not only can they not say no to others, they can't even say it to themselves. They are unwilling to admit that their time and energies are limited. Arbies, especially, want to be liked, and some of them feel that the way to please others is by doing things for them, so they consistently take on any comer. Too many people, therefore, "die from terminal niceness." They sabotage their own lives by constantly taking on too much. They work long hours and then still suffer from terrible tension, trying to figure out how to achieve all they've promised.

The irony is that those people who can't say no to unimportant matters inadvertently end up saying no to important things. They agree to almost anything—then, at the last minute, they may be forced to pull back out because they are physically incapable of fulfilling their promises.

> Betty's friend Jill was a person who couldn't say no. Jill and Betty would agree to play tennis at certain times and, because Betty was acutely aware of Jill's inability to turn anything down, she would say to Jill, "I'll meet you at the courts tomorrow at 4:00 P.M. Now, if you find you can't make it, please call me, because otherwise I'll play at the club during my regular time at 2:00 P.M." Jill would promise faithfully to be there or call. Then, at about 3:00 P.M., Jill would call Betty and beg off: "I couldn't sleep because I was so wound up from my meeting last night and then had that big appointment all morning. I'm sorry, but I'm just so tired I can't make it today." Although Jill valued her relationship with Betty immensely, Betty finally felt manipulated and cooled the friendship. If Jill had been able to say no to Betty (and to herself) initially, it would have been fine, but by waiting until the last minute and still having to say no, Jill alienated her best friend.

If you can't say no, you have to learn that you are not duty-bound to take on every project anyone suggests. This is a difficult concept for some to assimilate, but you must learn that, so long as you are doing a conscientious job, others will actually respect you for being more selective in choosing what to take on. This one conscious decision alone can start you on your path back to controlling your life.

The "Not to Do" List

Since deciding what *not* to do is just as important as deciding what to do, may we suggest making a *"not* to do" list? Each time you catch yourself doing nonproductive busywork during a time when you feel you could be accomplishing important work, or accepting tasks that are beyond your capabilities, make a note of that activity on your "not to do" list. Keep this list semipermanently—until you have firmly established in your mind what represents the busywork that is sabotaging your productive work.

Now, we aren't suggesting you have to give up doing these activities entirely. If there's something you enjoy doing, then plan to do it for recreation—or at least at a time when you don't feel you need to be accomplishing something. The key is to distinguish between what is productive work and what isn't. We want to emphasize that *we are not suggesting you should be "busy" doing productive work every minute of your life.* Quite the opposite, in fact. Our purpose in this book is to explain *how to get your work done in the most effective manner* [*so you'll have time to play*]—to do those things that are important to you for relationships, recreation, hobbies, or any other "downtimes" you might want to enjoy.

Left-Brain Overload

This is an appropriate time to discuss the need for all people, regardless of hemisphere dominance, to switch back and forth regularly between left- and right-brain activities.

There is a human need—an appetite, if you will—to use both sides of the brain. The extent of this need will be determined by the dominance of the individual, but everyone needs to use both sides. Using one side predominantly for too long can cause an overload, or burnout. Almost everyone is familiar with burnout—those times when you've worked on something intently, say recordkeeping, for about as long as you can stand it, and finally you want to stand up and scream—or something like that. (The authors occasionally experienced that phenomenon while writing this book, in fact.)

Right-brain burnout, however, receives less attention, yet it, too, is a normal occurrence. Everyone has heard stories about a person who simply "dropped out." Perhaps the person wandered aimlessly around the country for a while, until one day he or she suddenly felt the need to get back on solid ground, get a job, have a family, and "settle down." On an immediate basis, perhaps you've taken a relaxing vacation and are fully ready, by the time it's over, to get back to work. In this case your need for right-brain activity has been satisfied for a while, and your need to use your left brain returns.

Along these same lines, the benefits of the "coffee break" were firmly established back in the 1940s when efficiency experts found that workers' productivity was actually greater when they were given time off from work for a break in the midmorning and midafternoon. Perhaps the world's first coffee break occurred when God created the world and rested on the seventh day.

In a general sense, then, we emphasize the absolute necessity for people to switch back and forth from right- to left-brain activities on a regular basis. Factors that can lead to overload of the left brain (and a resulting inner need to switch to the right brain) include the following:

- an overload of words, arguments, or demands for concentration
- extreme physical exhaustion, comfort, or discomfort
- deprivation of food or sensory stimulation

(These and other factors are set out in the book *Whole Brain Thinking*, by Jacquelyn Wonder and Priscilla Donovan.)

Any of the above-mentioned catalysts can cause you to slide almost imperceptibly into a right-brain state. Depending on the severity of the overload, you may experience this glide to the right as something of a trance or hallucinatory state, a blurring of your thinking, or, on the lighter side, perhaps simply a need to talk to someone else, to laugh, to use your imagination, or any other right-brain activity.

Not only do Arbies slide much more willingly into the right-brain mode than do Elbies; they naturally experience left-brain overload more quickly, owing to their difficulties with, and resulting frustration at, left-brain activities.

Attitudes

Attitudes directly affect the choices we make, how much we accomplish, and ultimately how successful we are. You can change your life by changing your attitude. Someone said, "Altitude is determined by attitude." In other words, how successful you become is directly influenced by your attitudes.

Many people have a wonderful can-do attitude at work, but when they get home, all they want to do is kick off their shoes and let down their hair. They no longer want to police themselves into perfection; they want to relax, to let go, to "let it all hang out." This is not so strange when one considers that when Arbies are forced to maintain strict decorum and discipline during the workday, they have a greater need to switch to a more natural living mode when they return home. And, yes, you guessed it: a left-brain person, exposed to chaotic days with little structure—telephones ringing, constant interruptions, much clutter, and so forth—will have a greater need for peace, quiet, and tidiness—in other words, a maximum of order—after hours.

Both cases are understandable. But if they are carried to the extreme, relationships can be damaged by the Elbie who insists on perfection at home, or by the Arbie who rarely, if ever, cleans things up at home. Not only can relationships be damaged, but of course never cleaning up amounts to self-sabotage.

"I Can't"

We all have things we don't think we can do well—or even at all. One person will say "I can't draw," or "I can't do math," or "I can't do mechanical repairs." No doubt you can think of one or two things you think you can't do, in terms of organization. For instance, "I can't keep things put away," "I can't find things," or "I can't keep up on filing." Fill in two of your *can't*s here:

1. I can't _____ .
2. I can't _____ .

Now strike out the word *can't* and replace it with *don't* for the same two ideas:

1. I don't _____.
2. I don't _____.

(Realize that you really *can* do it, you just *don't* do it.)
Now replace *don't* with *won't*:

1. I won't _____.
2. I won't _____.

Become aware that you *don't* normally do it because you *won't* do it.

Does this give you new insight? You know you don't do it because you won't—you don't want to. Perhaps you've never given it a good try, or learned to do it properly.

Finally—and most important—replace *won't* with *can* and tell yourself:

1. I CAN _____.
2. I CAN _____.

Unless you are truly impaired, if other people can do it, you can, too, if you put your mind to it. Keep telling yourself "I can" instead of complaining that you can't. It may well be that the job is more difficult for you than for some others, but you are still capable of learning and growing. Give yourself credit for being the intelligent person you are.

"Just Quick" Do Your Work

Betty's best friend, Carol, lived across the street from her. Almost everything about Betty's and Carol's circumstances were similar: They were about the same age, came from similar backgrounds, practiced the same religion, had the same types of houses, and had small children.

There was one major difference, however. Carol would often make remarks such as "Oh, I just quick picked up the toys," or "I just quick ran some errands," or "I just quick wrote some checks."

And then there was Betty. Betty just *had* to get her vacuuming done. After several days of bemoaning that fact, she would finally open the closet, pull out the vacuum, attach the hose, attach the wand, select the attachment, and finally try to plug it in (the plug's prongs, of course, were always bent and never fit right, so she had to jiggle it to get it to stay just right). Well . . . by that time, she needed a cup of coffee.

It doesn't take long to do most things, yet we tend to build mountains out of molehills and drag our heels when it's time to do things we don't want to do. If you can approach your own work with a positive attitude, you, too, can "just quick" do your work.

SUMMARY

Two Reasons to Work on Something
> *1. It has a high priority.*
> *2. It is an irritant.*

Irritants
- *Identify your irritants.*
- *Realize how much less you'll feel you have to do, once they're handled.*
- *Is an irritant holding you back from accomplishing important goals in your life?*

The Domino Effect
- *Make a list of things you want to accomplish.*
- *Ask yourself what is holding you back from accomplishing them. Is there a "domino effect" involved?*

7

STARTING TO GET READY
TO THINK ABOUT . . .

The preceding chapters provide all you need to know to utilize effective goal-setting and time management. They will only help you, however, if you put that knowledge to work. Just thinking it's a good idea "to begin to start to prepare to get ready to think about considering the possibility" won't get the job done. The idea needs to be put into action. If you don't do anything about it—that is, *if you procrastinate*—then all you have read is useless.

As noted earlier, too many people use "I don't have time" as an excuse for not getting certain work done. The fact is, if you schedule your tasks and follow through, you may even have time left over. If you continually procrastinate, however, you'll endure a lifetime of never having "enough time." The aim of this chapter, then, is specifically to help you overcome procrastination. We believe our case study of George will reveal new insights into why you may delay your work, and we'll propose recommendations for overcoming this subtle problem.

George, the hospital director mentioned in Chapter 6, possessed great expertise in his field. Besides his master's degree in hospital administration from a leading university, he had many years of administrative experience, innovative ways of running his department, a knack for long-range planning, and an ability to track innumerable details in his head. Unfortunately, he felt stress most of the time.

He was like other people who procrastinate because they are not confident they have developed the skills to do what they need to get done. Because he perceived himself as incapable of handling certain tasks, he would wait until the last minute to do that work. Only the imminent approach of a deadline would pressure him to complete a project; thus he often worked late into the night. Since deadlines were frequent, so were his nights burning the midnight oil.

He muttered constantly about how much he had to do; yet, when he sat down to work, he invariably took the line of least resistance, making phone calls, zipping into a colleague's office to discuss an issue, or suddenly "needing" a cup of coffee.

It wasn't easy for a person like George to change his habits and gain control of his life, but in order for him to lower his blood pressure and reduce his stress, it was imperative.

PROCRASTINATION

People procrastinate for many reasons, but often they do so on tasks that make them uncomfortable—a result of lack of confidence in their ability to do the job in question. As was discussed earlier, you may simply be uncomfortable doing something that isn't natural for you. For instance, every intelligent person knows how to make a telephone call, but some believe they don't have the skills to handle certain situations well on the phone, and therefore will delay making all calls, or certain kinds of calls. It is often their *perception* (and therefore the comfort level) of their inability, rather than their intrinsic lack of skills, that causes people to hesitate.

The acronym "PUT OFF" can be used to summarize the specific causes of procrastination:

$P = Priority$

$U = Unknowns$

$T = Time$

$O = Overload$

$F = Fears$

$F = Feelings$

Priority

Placing the importance of certain tasks too low in your priorities is the first reason for not getting those tasks done. It's been our experience that Arbies, especially, tend to think that cleaning up and organizing is a complete waste of time (to say nothing of boring). Intellectually they know that a daily maintenance program would help them, and they may even practice setting aside a time every day for a few days to put things in order, but then the inevitable day comes when they are "too busy," and things begin to slide again.

This type of living—or working—can be referred to as a "slippery slide" existence because you work very hard to get everything put away—that is, you exert great effort to climb the steps to the top of the slippery slide—and everything looks great from that neat and lofty position. But no sooner do you get everything looking beautiful than you begin to let your areas become messy again, and soon you're sliding back "down to the pits." If you follow this pattern, your life can become nothing but a series of neat "ups" and chaotic "downs."

The importance of keeping your home or office tidy (daily maintenance) could be compared to the importance of keeping heavy equipment running.

If, for instance, a highway building crew doesn't take the time to ensure that their trucks and machinery are always in good running order—that is, if their tires, grease, oil, brakes, fluids, and so on aren't checked regularly—they will experience many breakdowns. When one piece breaks down, others are idled too, as well as costly crews who cannot work without their equipment. So construction companies (the ones who stay in business, anyway!) know well the importance of taking the time for daily maintenance.

Taking the time to put maintenance at a high enough priority—considering it an *investment* of time rather than a waste—prevents constant breakdowns in the form of time lost, as well as frustration and guilt from not being able to find things when needed, and perpetual embarrassment for not having a neat-looking office. Getting oneself to do such maintenance, though, may not be easy or natural. Many other routine tasks—from mailing greeting cards to doing one's income taxes—could be applied to the "too-low priority" rule as well. They may seem mundane and minor, but if you let them slide, they can create problems that are anything but minor.

Unknowns

The concept of *unknowns,* or inadequate information, is a real eye-opener for most people. If you take a look at the work you are delaying, you will probably find that many things you are putting off require some type of knowledge or information you don't have. Perhaps it's research for an analysis, and you don't know where to look for that information. Maybe, as mentioned earlier, it's a repair you don't know how to make—an expansion bolt that's fallen out of the wall, or a hole burned in your car seat. Or you may be delaying making a decision about whether to attend a seminar or whether your company should invest in certain technology.

Too many people get uptight about decisions, and don't realize it's a lack of information that's holding them up. They think only in terms like "I need to repair that hole," not "Where can find the information I need to learn how to repair that hole?" or "Where can I go to find someone to repair that hole for me?"

Also, it's important to gather a reasonable amount of data, and then make the best decision you can. *At one time or another, everyone has to make decisions based on inadequate information.* The higher a manager gets promoted in a corporation, the more risks he or she has to take by making decisions with partial information. Even the President of the United States has had to declare war on other countries with incomplete information. All he and the Congress could do was conduct as much research as possible and then make the best decision they could, based upon what they knew—right or wrong. Only God and the proverbial crystal ball always know what the exact outcome will be (and no one we've met yet has had a direct line to either one). The rest of us have to question the daylights out of everything, do the best we can, and, once the decision is made, know that we did the best we could with the information we had at the time. Second-guessing yourself afterwards is a waste of time and will diminish your confidence.

Time

Have you ever gotten up in the morning and shuffled through your bathroom collection of paraphernalia for shaving, shampooing, caring for your teeth, or putting on makeup, thinking, "I've got to clean this stuff out"? But you're still sleepy, you haven't had breakfast, and the day awaits you, so you tell yourself you'll "do it later." Several times that day you return to the same place, each time telling yourself you need to clean out that area, and each time you repeat excuses such as "I don't have time," "It's too late," or "I'm too tired." The next morning you stumble back into your bathroom, where the identical scenario is repeated once again. Suddenly you realize, "This is a recording!"

This happens because *you have not set aside a specific time* to clean it out. Chances are good that once you got that task inscribed in your schedule, you would actually be willing to do it. Without a written reminder, though, it's a case of "out of sight, out of mind"—especially if you're visually oriented and might never think of it again, once you leave the room. Therefore we recommend keeping a pad and pencil in the bathroom—and one by the bed, by each phone, in your purse or pocket, on your desk, and anywhere else you frequent, so that you can immediately jot down your idea at that moment.

Once a note is written, you need to establish a procedure for ensuring that such reminders reach your planning area, where they can then be included in your schedule. Simply placing them in your pocket, in a certain spot in your room, or even on the floor of your doorway (assuming you really will pick them back up and take them with you) can be very effective in helping you remember to take them along. (See Chapter 4.)

Whether it's cleaning out a dresser drawer, purging file drawers, or backing up computer files, it probably won't get done unless you set aside a specific time to do it.

Overload

People tend to overestimate the time it takes to do work they dislike, and underestimate the time to do things they enjoy. Especially if you are an Arbie and you don't care much about time anyway, if you are involved in something you relish doing—be it an art or a craft, casual reading, shopping, dancing, or daydreaming, time can whiz by and you're likely to find yourself running late. On the other hand, you can look at a pile of clothes on your bedroom floor and perceive that it will take an hour to clean up. This, of course, would be an overload on your schedule, but in reality it might not take more than five or ten minutes.

George, the hospital director mentioned at the beginning of this chapter, had to learn to be more realistic about how much time it would take to accomplish all the projects he willingly accepted (which he generally estimated too low) and then later be realistic about how long it would in fact take him to do them (which he usually estimated too high).

Setting aside irrational fears about the overwhelming size of a task will calm your emotions and let you be realistic. Making a mountain out of a molehill causes stress and is self-defeating. To avoid overload, it's much easier to break the task down into steps and "chew off" one bit at a time, as discussed in Chapter 4.

Fear of Failure (or Success)

Perfectionists have a particularly difficult time in life, and there is a broad spectrum of perfectionism.

For instance, there are the "perfect perfectionists." As mentioned in Chapter 1, everything about them and their environment is perfect. There is never a wrinkle in their clothing, their desks and file drawers are perfectly neat and tidy, their cars are always sparkling, and so on. Even if they are left-brain-dominant people, some (but not all) of these "perfect perfectionists" live in a continual state of exhaustion from trying to do everything perfectly. If they are naturally right-brain-dominant people who have had perfectionism hammered into their psyches by their parents from the day they were born, they are probably extremely tense people, too. They live in constant stress, not only because of their deep belief that "you shouldn't do anything unless you do it right", but because being perfect is unnatural to them. They feel, despite their constant efforts, that they are never living up to others' expectations, and therefore they constantly feel like failures. This fear of failure, then, causes them to dread their work, because failure is simply beyond their own acceptable limits.

As an example of a "perfect perfectionist," a participant in a seminar conducted by one of the authors announced she was excited about creating a written reminder system as described in the session the week before. She had studied the system and thought it was a great idea, and *just as soon as she bought the right calligraphy pen* to write notes to herself, she was going to set it up . . .

At the opposite end of the perfectionism spectrum are "imperfect perfectionists." These people have also been taught to do things right or not at all, but their perception of their capabilities is so low that they feel they cannot succeed at anything—so they don't try. The sad result is utter chaos. Their hair, clothes, homes, children, cars, and desks are all unkempt. They are emotionally blocked and therefore paralyzed from attempting almost any action because of their fear of failure. They also fear success, because being successful doesn't fit their self-image. This type of person could benefit from counseling to gain self-esteem and function more effectively.

Between the polarized ends of the perfectionism spectrum, however, is a broad range of very normal people who may exhibit an "odd couple" variety of perfectionism about certain things and not others. A man may tend to rewrite typed business letters endlessly, but his handwritten interoffice notes may be almost illegible.

It has been our experience that Arbies fall into the trap of being perfectionistic about right-brain endeavors, but not about left-brain activities. A woman may be an absolute perfectionist when it comes to the interior decorating of her home, yet her papers may be crammed into paper bags on her closet floors and in innumerable other nooks and crannies throughout the house—anywhere, so long as they are out of sight.

If you're a perfectionist, of whatever kind, remember that it's a waste of time to spend, as the saying goes, "a hundred dollars' worth of time on a ten-cent item." That same time could be spent much more productively (if less enjoyably) doing something else that's more important in the whole scheme of life.

Perfectionists should also realize that it's often better to do a task half-right than not at all. They need to learn to forgive themselves for not doing it perfectly. They usually need an authority figure to say, "It's all right. Just do your best and leave it at that." In fact, we, the authors, hereby give you permission to do just that!

Feelings

Emotional discomfort is the sixth and final reason people procrastinate. Both Elbies and Arbies tend to have difficulty in this area, but for different reasons. Susan, for instance, dreaded doing evaluations because she sometimes had to tell her employees they weren't working up to expectations in certain areas—something most people, of course, would rather avoid. Giving negative feedback was extremely painful for her.

Elbies, on the other hand, might feel less emotion and can therefore more or less "coldheartedly" handle that same problem. However, giving positive feedback, such as complimenting an employee on exceptional performance, might be more uncomfortable for an Elbie, while Arbies may enjoy complimenting, counseling, or nurturing their subordinates. Discomfort with expressing intimate feelings might appear in an inability to write letters, greeting cards, and especially thank-you notes.

One young woman admitted privately after a seminar that she had not sent out thank-you notes for her wedding gifts. Upon questioning, she reluctantly disclosed she had been married for two years, and the situation was causing a great deal of anxiety in her life, yet she could not bring herself to finish this task. In further discussions, we learned that this woman had been raised in a lower-income family, while her husband's parents' friends—the ones who had sent so many nice gifts—were quite affluent. It turned out that she didn't feel equal to these people and therefore was reticent to address them, even in the form of a thank-you note. Two years later she still had not mailed those notes and still felt bad about it. To this day we feel sad for her. She needs to either mail those notes or decide they are no longer important, in order to let the emotional upset go. Until she does one or the other, she will continue to carry her guilt.

Whether it's a debt that needs to be repaid, a broken relationship that requires mending, or a relationship that needs to be broken because it's not in your best interests, the sooner you right the situation, the sooner you'll feel better about it.

Ask "Why?"

If you don't really understand why you are delaying doing a certain task, ask yourself this simple question: "Why am I putting it off?"

No doubt the reason you'll give yourself will be "Because I don't want (or don't like) to do it." Fair enough.

Now ask yourself, "What is it about the task I don't like or want to do?" At that point, go back over these six reasons:

1. *Do I consider it a low-priority task (when it's not one)?*
2. *Do I have all the information necessary to make a decision?*
3. *Have I set aside a specific time to do it?*
4. *Does it seem overwhelming? (Break it down into units if it does.)*

If, after asking these four questions, you still can't figure out why you are postponing the task, ask yourself:

5. *What has kept me from achieving it?* Many times this will bring you to a new realization that you don't know how to do it, or some other reason mentioned above. Being honest with yourself by admitting to, and dealing with, your frailties is the first step in overcoming weaknesses and regaining control of your life.

Next, ask yourself:

6. *What steps will it take to achieve this task?* It may be that you'll need to do a lot of preparation for a little task, and maybe the "domino effect" is involved—as it was with our friend Carol, who was delaying getting carpet because she didn't know whom to get to putty her windows.

Once you've identified your roadblocks and the steps you need to take, write down those steps and then schedule each item in order. This is difficult, of course, and totally unnatural for an Arbie, but it's the most effective way to ensure that your work gets done.

SUMMARY

- *Busywork may be used to avoid facing important responsibilities.*
- *Focusing can be difficult because it involves eliminating some of the possible choices and accepting limitations.*
- *Engaging in left- or right-brain activities for too long can cause an overload that can be alleviated by a switch to activities involving the opposite side.*
- *If something is an irritant, or if it's an activity that will help you reach a goal, then it deserves your immediate attention.*
- *Set aside ten minutes per day to get rid of irritants.*
- *When you are experiencing the "domino effect," think through what your roadblock is, and prioritize the steps to be taken.*
- *If you are delaying certain work, ask yourself if any of the following factors are involved:*

  Priority (too low?)
  Unknowns (inadequate information?)
  Time (scheduled?)
  Overload (perceived?)
  Fears (of failure or success)
  Feelings (avoiding personal interaction)

- *Remember that it's more important to be productive than to be perfect.*

8

THE CLUTTERBUG

THE LAW OF THE CLUTTERBUG

*Clutter expands to fill the areas
allowed for its reception.*

Just as important as getting your time under control is getting your possessions under control—which in turn will save you time.

For a left-brain person, an organized workspace means a neat and tidy working area with a place for everything and everything in its place. The same may not hold true for you, however. Since Arbies enjoy having many things going on at once—requiring the use of innumerable objects—they have a different definition of the word *organized*. You can assess your own "clutter quotient" with two simple questions:

- Can I find what I need?
- Am I (and the people I live or work with) comfortable with my pace?

If the answer to both questions is yes, then you feel organized. If the answer to both questions is no, then you know a change needs to be made.

"Aunt Jennie," as she is affectionately known to all the kids on the block, thinks she has room for everyone and everything in her house. A warm and cheerful soul, she welcomes you into her home, even if she has to clear off a chair for you to sit on. A bustling sort of woman, she has collected every sort of object—trinkets from her grandchildren, greeting cards she's received, and so forth.

Her husband has passed away, and now she has decided to move into an apartment. She's spent the last several months sorting through her lifetime of belongings, but somehow there is no end in sight. Everything is so precious to her that parting with anything is difficult. She called us, saying, "I don't know where to begin. Every time I look around, I see things with sentimental value, and even the stuff I don't want to keep, I'm sure someone could use."

Jennie wondered at the fact that she had spent the first half of her life accumulating possessions—and now she has been spending the second half of it trying to figure out what to do with them! Because she's elderly, she feels time is limited, which creates a conflict because she doesn't want her heirs to have to deal with her belongings. "On the other hand," she mused, "if I have only a few years left to live, do I want to spend all my time dealing with this?"

The Need for Clutter

In a sense, Arbies like Jennie have a *need* for clutter. Too much neatness seems sterile and suggests formality rather than their spontaneous style. Since formality causes them discomfort, they feel more relaxed when surrounded by clutter.

People like Aunt Jennie enjoy creating "nests"—places where they can surround themselves with all of their own paraphernalia, places in which they create their own private world. This area may be a bedside reading area, an office, a workshop, or their whole living or working area—places where things are arranged in casual but oh-so-comfortable surroundings. They usually know where everything is, and they feel warm and cozy when they are there, no matter how uninviting it looks to others. Sometimes, though, these nests accumulate so much clutter that it becomes a problem to the person herself.

The Cost of Clutter

There's nothing wrong with having a fondness for clutter, but when clutter gets out of control, it becomes an aggravation rather than a source of comfort. The monetary, physical, and mental cost of trying to accomplish anything in the midst of a great deal of clutter is great. Conversely, if your things are conveniently stored for easy use and are not in the way to hide other items or act as distractions, you can accomplish your work much more quickly and effectively.

There's a saying in manufacturing that "a clean, quiet factory produces low-cost, high-quality products, while a dirty, noisy environment produces low-quality, high-cost products." The same is true in an office or home environment. Besides that, you may find the clutter itself upsetting—especially if you live or work with others who make an issue of it.

Do you have at least one isolated spot in your home or office where nothing—we mean *nothing*—is allowed to accumulate? It might be an attractive coffee table and two chairs reserved for guests in your office. At home it might be the front entry, the dining room table, or perhaps the lovely antique table you inherited from your grandmother. That place is sacrosanct—a place you wouldn't even *think* of piling up miscellaneous junk.

Now take a minute to consider the places you *do* allow clutter to collect. It may be on your office windowsill, the top of your credenza, or perhaps one or more "junk drawers" in your desk. At home it might be around your favorite reading spot, the back entry, your desk, the attic, or the basement.

Why does one spot accumulate "stuff" while another doesn't? The simple answer is that you *allowed* it to collect there. In the same way that doing nothing is a decision about what to do, it was actually a *decision* you made whether or not you would allow clutter to collect, and where.

If you are tired of having certain areas continually cluttered, realize that you can make a *conscious decision* not to allow things to collect there, and they won't. Realize when you make that decision, however, that your things will have to go somewhere, and substituting one catchall for another won't solve your problem. Instead, along with your vows not to allow clutter to accumulate, you're going to have to spend a little time creating some easy and natural-to-use places to store the items that ordinarily land in the places you're trying to clear.

Distractions

It's very distracting to work in a cluttered area. Especially if you're visually oriented, you are tempted with each and every "sighting" to do a different task, instead of focusing on what you are already doing. If you're coaxed into distractions regularly—taking just one stitch in your needlepoint or tapping just one more nail into your carpentry project (either of which may stretch into several stitches or nails)— be creative. Make a game out of making distractions magically disappear by putting them out of sight: If newspaper or magazine headlines plead to be read, if crossword puzzles beckon, if candy bars look inviting, put your distractions out of your view so that you can find them if you want them, but you won't notice them as you move about.

Besides being distracting, working in a cluttered area is inefficient. Not only is it difficult to spread out and utilize the space you need; it's also difficult to find materials you may need. Some individuals actually make the situation worse when they go looking for something. Filing folders may be pulled out, left open, and not replaced, stacks of paper may be left lying. Not too many people do this, but if you are one of these "search and destroy" types, stop to consider how much difficulty you are causing yourself.

Keeping It Clean

As Don Aslett, author of several books on cleaning, points out, it's much easier to *keep* a place clean than to *get* it clean. If you tend to sweep everything into your desk drawer when you leave your office and the next day pull out only what you need, things will collect in that drawer that you'll never see again.

The old cliché about cleaning up for the cleaning lady holds great wisdom. The person who gets rid of clutter in preparation for a cleaning service is smart indeed. If there's a lot of clutter, a janitorial service or house cleaner will only have time to straighten and clean the much-used areas, without ever getting to the corners. A cleaning person may also charge more to clean space that is cluttered.

Though a cleaning service can be very helpful, it can never solve your organizational problems. Cleaning people can straighten and clean, but they cannot make decisions about what to keep or throw away, or properly clean out and purge your desk drawers. Consequently, a cleaning service may only camouflage the underlying problems.

Imagine a room with no windows, furniture, drapes, carpet, or clutter, and guess how long it would take to clean it. Now add windows, drapes, an area rug, and furniture, and consider how much longer it would now take to clean the same room. Add first a little clutter, then a large amount of clutter, and again consider the time and effort needed to clean it properly. You can now understand the importance of simplifying your life by weeding out as much excess as possible.

SAVERS

Over the years we have noted a persistent, striking phenomenon in our organizing seminars: About ninety-seven percent of our attendees admit they are "savers." While numerous other factors also contribute, *being a saver is the single greatest cause of disorganization,* and one of the best ways to simplify your life is to get rid of extra "stuff."

Unfortunately, saving things is a right-brain trait. While Elbies can often coldheartedly pitch out whatever they don't need, Arbies tend to become emotionally attached to their belongings and have difficulty parting with them.

Look around your home or office. How many items do you have? Did you know you could easily have more than 200,000 items in your home? Think of all the paper clips, individual papers, hobby or recreational equipment, socks, belts, ties, and scarves (many of which you never wear). If you have more "stuff" than the average person, you are a saver.

There are several problems incurred by being a saver. First, it's easy to run out of storage space. Second, if you're a poor decision maker, you can't decide where to keep items, and they tend to stack up in piles that become cluttered. This, in turn, causes disorganization, and soon time can be lost in trying to find things.

The Cost of Storing "Stuff"

Although most people will readily admit it if they are savers, what most do not consider is that everything they keep—even items in storage—costs time, energy, and maintenance. Storage space costs money—even if it's in your attic or supply room. Would you pay five dollars in rent per shelf to store the stuff you have there? With fewer possessions, could you live or work in a smaller—and therefore less expensive—building? Many people actually pay rent for remote storage facilities to store possessions they don't use or need. Possessions must be maintained—washed, filed, repaired, dusted, shuffled from one place to another, accounted for, and yes, even sometimes agonized over at times when trying to decide what to do with them.

Items That Have No Use

To make matters even worse, people save things for which they have no use. One example is the familiar story of the woman who had a box, neatly tied and labeled PIECES OF STRING TOO SHORT FOR ANY USE!

Some people retain "expensive mistakes"—objects that cost a great deal of money and that they don't really like, want, or use. However, since the cost was great, they are reluctant to dispose of these items. "This is a very expensive picture" the owner maintains staunchly, even though he doesn't like the art object, it serves no purpose, and it is packed away in a storage area.

Other people keep things with the thought that eventually they'll create ways to use them. As if they weren't already busy enough, they hang on to items seemingly for the express purpose of making more work for themselves in the future! Trying to *create a use for an item for which you have no use is the world's greatest waste of time.*

Worst of all, as collections build, it can become a seemingly insurmountable task to purge belongings. Their owners find themselves overwhelmed with a task they don't want to face, and they can't relax or enjoy their deserved time off because they constantly feel guilty about the huge number of chores that await them. Pam, a woman in one of our seminars, related that her husband came home from work one day with the exciting announcement that he felt sure their lifetime dream of being transferred to Europe could happen in only two more years. Her immediate reaction was one of panic: "I'll never be ready on time!" she thought.

Unless you have too much time on your hands (and few people do, these days), if you have an item for which you have no use, repeat to yourself over and over "enough is enough" and then *get rid of it.*

Beliefs, Culture, and Personality Traits

Our society has been deeply influenced by the way our country has developed. From the hardships of the immigrants and pioneers who settled the prairies, through the adversities of the Depression era and the rationing of World War II, the idea that we must conserve and "make good use" of our resources has been thoroughly ingrained in us. Many of us have been taught to "save for a rainy day." After all, you "never know" when you might need an item. And besides that, "life is too good, and you never know when our bubble is going to burst" and "things won't be so good anymore." But even on that rainy day, how many butter tubs, plastic sacks, worn-out sneakers, sets of painting clothes, reference files, or unread periodicals are you going to need? Making the best use of your resources might mean keeping your kitchen cupboard manageable instead of cramming it with potentially useful stuff.

We're not putting down savers—in fact, we particularly enjoy working with savers because they have many appealing personality traits; they tend to be honest, frugal, earnest, "salt-of-the-earth" types who believe that if you don't need something, surely someone else can "make good use of it." So they save it until they can find a proper recipient.

Unfortunately, what they don't seem to consider is that as long as they have it, no one else can use it! The items need to be moved on to a resale shop, a charitable organization, a recycling center, or some other place where people who need them can find them.

Ecology

The ecological movement has raised our consciousness about the importance of not continually adding to our bulging landfills. The environmentally aware have now added incentive not to toss unneeded items into the trash flow. Instead, many people now tend to hang on to even more of these unwanted items with the good intentions of recycling them. Unfortunately, it's their homes or offices that begin to bulge, rather than the landfills.

The problem is that we've been trained to save, *but we've never been trained how to deal with what we've saved.* Our forefathers saved because they had so few material possessions. Nowadays the problem is just the opposite. We can no longer continue to accumulate possessions or they will eventually inundate us.

Insecurities

Personal insecurity is another reason people save things. The more insecure a person is, the more he or she clings to possessions. The toddler's "security blanket" is a classic example, and as people mature they replace their "blankie" with other comforting possessions such as trophies, retired shoes, old records, and unfinished projects.

The fear of parting with sentimental possessions causes particular problems, and the reason we don't want to let things go is difficult to identify.

> As an adult, our friend Stacy needed to have two teeth extracted in preparation for wearing braces, but suddenly she experienced unreasonable fears. When

she shared these feelings with her dentist, he explained that it wasn't unusual to experience anxiety about letting go of teeth that were a part of her body.

We have also noted a sense of loss in some of our clients' anxiety over parting with possessions that they have allowed to become emotional parts of themselves. In this process they actually seem to go through experiences of denial, argument, bargaining, depression, and finally acceptance. These stages are similar to those identified by author Elisabeth Kübler-Ross in accepting any kind of loss in our lives, large or small.

Savers will often deny the need to dispose of some of their possessions. When another person suggests that these objects must go, they may react with anger or hostility. "These things are perfectly good," the owner argues. Or, "Leave my stuff alone!"

Following that is often a bargaining period before the person finally admits resignedly that there really isn't reason to keep the items anymore. Finally the person accepts the "loss" and allows the items to go.

In fact, having once dealt with the matter, the person is usually much happier to have it done—which would indicate that it was the process of *deciding* to let go that was so painful, not the loss of the items in themselves. In fact, once they're gone, these items are rarely thought of again.

CAUSES OF CLUTTER

If your office or home is cluttered, look around and ask yourself why things are lying around. There are four usual reasons why an item is left out:

1. It's a reminder. If you tend to be visually oriented, you may be afraid that if you put it away you will forget to do it. Perhaps it's a letter that needs to be answered, a book that needs to be returned to the library, the address of a business person you need to contact, or mending that needs to be done.

Because half-finished projects often fall into this category, let's pause to consider them, as well. Projects often remain unfinished for a variety of reasons—most often because you have lost enthusiasm for the project. Perhaps it's not turning out as well as you'd like, or you don't enjoy working on it as much as you had anticipated, or life has inundated you with too many other responsibilities. Leonardo da Vinci, for instance, had a terrible record of not finishing his projects. When he died, it was discovered that he had left many more paintings unfinished than he had ever finished!

This is another kind of thing that even normally truthful people tend to deceive themselves about. We repeatedly tell ourselves we'll "get around to it soon," though we know full well that we'll always be able to think of something better to do.

Be honest with yourself and get rid of unfinished projects you don't like, want, or need. For those projects you really *will* finish, find an appropriate storage space for them and make a note to yourself where you stored them, then *schedule the time to finish them on your calendar*—even if it's two years from now.

2. It's Difficult to Put Away. Another reason things sit out is that they're inconvenient to put away. If an item such as a children's game is played in the living room but stored in the child's room upstairs, there's a high likelihood that the child won't be inclined to put it away when he's finished playing with it. If a file drawer is already too full, filing more papers in it will seem like a difficult job—which it is. If bowls are stacked too deep in the bottom of the kitchen cabinet, a person may be tempted, instead of putting them away, just to put them on the counter with the promise, "I'll put them away later."

Creating an easy-to-use place for storing items—especially those used by children—will increase the likelihood of their being put away, and less clutter will tend to accumulate.

3. Lack of Decision-making. *One of the most frequently overlooked reasons for disorganization is that many people have trouble making decisions.* If you can't decide where to put something, the temptation is to find a temporary resting place, such as dropping a paper on a stack on your desk "for now," putting magazines you want to give away in your garage, or moving a piece of unneeded furniture to the basement "just until we decide what to do with it." Author Don Aslett calls these places "indecision spots," and the sad fact is that items may literally sit there for years.

4. No Place Established. If no place has been established to store certain items, you won't know what to do with them. Loose papers with no apparent connection are particularly difficult to deal with. Personal letters that you want to answer, photos for which you have inadequate albums, brochures you may want to refer to, and so on, tend to pile up in stacks or be tucked in corners here and there. Odd items, such as extra ashtrays, videotapes, scarves, mittens, receipts, and trophies, have a way of sitting around without "homes."

Unfortunately, it takes analytical/engineering types of skills to build and design organizing tools. Closed-in storage spaces such as filing cabinets, cupboards, cabinets, and closets are created by left-brain people *for* left-brain people. Because these places aren't natural for Arbies to use, items get left out instead. Arbies need direct visibility of and accessibility to, their possessions. Since uncovered storage reveals not only objects but a more cluttered appearance, it's difficult to achieve both neatness and instant accessibility.

Arbies prefer storage that can be left open for normal usage, but can be quickly and easily closed or covered up. Examples would be a roll-top desk, or the standard piece of furniture called a secretary. Exposed filing cabinets with slide-back covers, such as those commonly used in doctors' offices, would serve as another example of this type of storage unit. Regardless of which type of storage you choose, it's vital that you create a place for your possessions that's easy to use.

SUMMARY

- *Ask yourself two simple questions: Can I find what I need? Am I comfortable with my workspace?*
- *Determine what amount of clutter is comfortable for you and those around you.*
- *Decide if keeping certain things is worth the monetary, physical, and mental cost of maintaining it.*
- *Don't waste time on items that have no use.*
- *Create a game out of making distractions just magically disappear.*
- *Be prepared to face a sense of loss as you let go of certain possessions. The sense of relief you feel afterwards will compensate for the feeling of loss.*
- *Put away items left out as reminders, including half-finished projects, and write a reminder to yourself.*
- *Create an easy-to-use place for storing items to increase the likelihood of their being put away.*
- *Make a conscious decision not to allow things to collect.*

9

TO KEEP OR NOT TO KEEP

Keeping physical clutter under control whether it's at home or at the office, is a huge step toward *feeling* organized, which of course is the first component of *being* organized. So in the next several chapters we'll discuss how to manage first possessions, then papers.

DIGGING OUT: FIRST STEPS

Your digging-out process will be easier and more effective if you first give some thought to the project, so here are some considerations:

Break the Job Down into Units

The idea of sorting out and reorganizing everything stored in a large office or a six-room house can be overwhelming—especially for the Arbie who sees the "whole" of everything. Since you can't do everything at once, there's only one way to tackle this weighty problem, and that is to break the job down into units. Ignore the big, overall project and "think small"—think in *units*. You can choose one of two approaches:

1. Start with one unit (the entry closet near the front door, perhaps), then move to the next unit (a cupboard). When that's done, move methodically through your home or office until everything's sorted out.

2. Start with your greatest irritant. Sometimes it's a relief to get irritants out of the way quickly, so you can go ahead and concentrate on bigger tasks.

Ideally, we'd recommend being methodical by starting at one place and moving around each room, then on to the next, and so on. But you may not agree—which is okay, so long as you get the job done. You may prefer to "blitz" the front hall closet or the medicine cabinet so they won't be looming over your head, then tackle the rest of whatever units you can manage.

Perhaps today you'll only do one small shelf. That's okay. Tomorrow you can clear off the shelf above that, and the day after you can do the shelf above that. So long as you're making progress, leaving things in better shape instead of leaving a trail of half-finished work behind you, that's what counts.

Divide your big organizing jobs into small units, and they won't seem so overwhelming.

Settle Territorial Disputes

Sandra Felton, founder of Messies Anonymous, first taught us this next worthwhile tip: Settle territorial disputes. In other words, don't start organizing other people's possessions without their permission. Nearly everyone has plenty of his or her own stuff to organize before getting around to anyone else's.

> Darlene's very first organizing activity was to organize her kitchen counter. After it was completed, she saw (after years of blaming her husband for the messes in their home) that none of the stuff on the kitchen counter was his—it was all hers! She realized for the first time that she had plenty of her own territory to cover before tackling his.

The above story illustrates why we caution people to attend organizing classes to improve *their own* organizing, not someone else's.

The ABCs of Accomplishing a Task

Whether you're cleaning a room at home or confronting a serious clutter problem at your place of business, you can accomplish a great deal in a short amount of time if you follow the ABCs of accomplishing tasks:

A. Anticipate your needs. Just like the Boy Scouts, "be prepared" by anticipating in advance what you'll need to get a certain job done. For cleaning, you'll need a vacuum, dust cloths, trash bags, etc.

B. Bar the door! Don't leave your work station until you're done with your assigned job. Pretend there are iron bars on the door and that it can only be opened when the task is complete.

Yes, you'll have interruptions that must be attended to, but if that happens, pretend there's a giant rubber band attached to the back of your shirt. You may get called to your boss's office, have to answer the door or the telephone, or attend to a crying baby, but the instant you're finished, that rubber band is going to zap you back where you were. (Otherwise there's a danger that when you leave your chore you'll become distracted with something else and not return to what you were doing.)

Imagine you're cleaning a family room. When you find something that must be returned to another room—drinking glasses to the kitchen, shoes to the bedroom, dirty socks to the laundry room—put all of these items together in one place near the door. They can be stacked on the floor or put on a chair or table—the place isn't important. What is important is that you put them in one designated spot and delay delivering *any* of them until you've finished cleaning that room. Then, and only then, make one delivery trip throughout the house to return items to their proper places.

C. Concentrate only on the task at hand! Because of the distractability of Arbies, it's especially important to remember to do *only what you set out to do.* It's all too easy, when you're cleaning out a stack of magazines, for instance, to become involved in reading an article rather than concentrating on the task at hand. (Elbies sometimes do this, too!)

One way to stay focused is to pretend you are your own supervisor, and plan the exact work you want your employee to do. Then pretend you're the employee and follow your "supervisor's" instructions without distractions. In the case of cleaning the family room, you can pretend you're a hired cleaning person who is to stick to straightening, vacuuming, and dusting *only.* When you notice a stack of magazines that needs sorting, jot that sorting task down as a reminder and schedule a time to sort them *after* you've finished cleaning that room and have put away your cleaning equipment. This approach may be difficult for you if you delight in having several things going at once. The Arbie alternative would be to choose two or three tasks to do at once while still incorporating the ABC technique.

The ABC method works for any type of task, but it will be especially useful while trying to "dig out" from under accumulated belongings.

INDECISION

Now it's time to get down to the nitty-gritty, the hardest part of all: decisions about what to keep and what to dispose of.

Many people who have trouble getting organized aren't even aware that they possess one very common trait: *difficulty in making decisions*. Arbies tend to be more confounded by decision-making because of divergent thinking; they simply generate many more possibilities. The analysis of these options is a left-brain skill.

When Kristine, one of our clients, began to get organized, she started by cleaning off her kitchen counter. She vowed to make decisions about each item as she came to it. One of those objects was a little paperweight her husband had brought home from a business meeting. Until that moment she had never looked closely at it. Now, however, she scrutinized it more carefully. It was a small marble base holding a Y-shaped vertical metal piece. Suspended from the arms of the Y was a disk that could be spun with the flick of a finger. On one side of this disk was etched the front half of a running horse and jockey, and the rear half of the figure appeared on the opposite side.

Then she noticed that a plaque on the base was inscribed DECISIONS, DECISIONS, DECISIONS. Suddenly she understood: It was a decision-maker! It was made to "flip the coin" and let "heads" or "tails" make decisions for you. Finally she appreciated the irony: That little "decision-maker" was sitting on her counter because she had been unable to make a decision about what to do with it! It taught her a lesson.

When you have a small decision to make, whichever way you decide won't affect your life much one way or the other. Don't worry about it—flip a coin and get on with your life!

Large Decisions

For larger decisions, there is a more ponderous system you can use. Let's briefly consider that system and then move on to a simpler method of decision-making:

1. Set out your goals. At one time our friend Darlene considered the possibility of moving to Australia, so she went down to her basement, surveyed the mountains of belongings stored there, and asked herself this question: If I were to pay to move myself to Australia, how much of this stuff would I take along? The answer, of course, was almost nothing, except for her suitcases.

Set out your goals by asking yourself how completely you want to attack getting your place in order. Do you want to just clean out a little, or do you want to get really serious and clean out everything you wouldn't pay to move to Australia?

If you're cleaning out your office, would you be willing to pay to move some of those things to an elegant new office building? If not, then you probably don't want to keep them here, either.

2. List the facts. What are your needs and those of your business or family? Do you have space available to keep excess stuff, or will it cost you more money to add storage space?

3. Consider the alternatives. Watch for duplications. Do you really still need that old typewriter since you've gotten your new computer? How many pots and pans can you use? Could you rent bulky equipment to do a certain once-a-year project, rather than letting it take up vital space?

4. Weigh the pros and cons and choose, based on the above priorities. Perhaps you could make a pro-and-con sheet of something of great import and study those points carefully before making important decisions.

Simplifying Decision-Making

Most decisions, however, just aren't that critical. Here are some easier questions that might help you simplify your decision-making:

1. How long since I used this item? Am I saving it for a "rainy day"? These are standard questions that anyone who's "digging out" needs to answer. If the object has been in storage a long time and you haven't used it in six months or a year, you'll probably never need it again, so you can let it go.

A storm had caused a power outage in Judy's neighborhood, and her family had no heat. They did have a wood-burning fireplace, but they were out of firewood. Judy was getting chilled, and she racked her brain to think of what they could burn to keep warm.

Suddenly she remembered a big box of scrap wood she and her husband had kept in their basement for their children to practice their carpentry skills. The children were now grown, and this offered her the perfect opportunity to get rid of the dusty box of wood. When she posed the idea to her husband, however, he steadfastly refused to burn the wood scraps because (you guessed it!) they "might need it sometime."

It's easy to shake our heads and laugh at others, but we need to look around at our own environments before we laugh too loudly. Like almost everyone else, you probably have at least some useless items stored in your home or office that you never use. Our advice? Get rid of them!

2. Can I justify keeping it? Is the item in question *earning* a place in your life? Belongings need to serve some purpose in order to be kept. Looking beautiful counts, as well as sentimental value (within limits). But what you paid for it does *not* count! Too many people retain possessions because they "paid a lot of money for it." However, it turns out that the object—a piece of furniture, for instance—was really just an expensive mistake. The monetary value of any item is only that for which you could sell it.

Because taking such a loss is difficult to accept, too many people would rather keep an object than sell it for so much less, even though it represents an irritant every time they look at it.

One man was pining for an expensive piece of fishing equipment that he didn't feel he could justify buying—until it occurred to him that he could sell a lot of his old, unused fishing gear at a garage sale and then use that money to purchase his coveted electronic depth-finder. (He's catching more fish these days, too!)

There's a reason you've quit using something. As Don Aslett says, it's outdated, broken, unsafe, replaced, out of style, un-attractive, inoperable, rusty—or perhaps you simply don't like it. Believe us when we tell you it won't get any better in the future.

3. What will happen if it's gone? If the answer is "Nothing," then let it go! Fear of making a mistake is a big factor in not disposing of items. Even if it's an unwanted gift or junk mail, the item has come into your ownership and now you are re-sponsible for it. Since making a mistake is unacceptable, this becomes a great deterrent to getting rid of it.

More often, however, people argue that the minute they get rid of something, they invariably need it soon after, so let's discuss that issue. The fact is, it's worth making two mistakes out of one hundred such decisions if you are freed of the other ninety-eight! We doubt that anything you mistakenly dispose of will greatly affect the quality of your life. Consider these minor errors as payment for the serenity you are enjoying by getting rid of the other ninety-eight items. Besides, if you in-advertently sell something you wanted at your own garage sale, you can always go to someone else's sale and buy another one just like it.

Also, people often want something they've just disposed of simply because it's fresh on their minds. (If they hadn't just given it away, they might have forgotten they had it in the first place and gone out and bought another one anyway!)

A last thought on this subject: It's okay to make a few mis-takes in life. Remember that the only people who don't make mistakes are the ones who don't do anything.

4. Is it an irritant? This last question needs to be answered honestly. *Would you feel better if you didn't have the item anymore?* Remember that every time you decide to keep an object, you'll be faced with that same decision again next time. However, *once you're rid of the item, you'll never have to deal with it again!* That alone makes getting rid of some items worthwhile.

Right or wrong, be *decisive*. Make these little decisions as you come to them. They won't make much difference either way, so relax, and move on to more important things.

Sentimental Items

People cling to sentimental items for a multitude of reasons—one being simply to prove they've "been there." Arbies are particularly prone to saving things in general—and sentimental items in particular—because of their tendency to become emotionally attached to their belongings.

We suggest that you rethink how many greeting cards, crutches, records from your teenage years, corsages, trophies, or other nostalgic items you want to keep. *It is all right to save an appropriate number of mementos,* but when you have saved so many that they become an irritant to you, you know it's time to weed some of them out in order to reduce your stress level.

Now this is a touchy subject, so we'll attempt to help clarify your thinking. The real question is, do you really enjoy looking back over these items periodically, or do you just harbor them, shunting them from place to place? If you truly do enjoy looking over them every once in a while, then by all means keep them. If you've saved every greeting card you've ever received, however, we suggest that the next time you go through them, you start weeding out all but those that are truly meaningful to you and let the rest go. Maybe you can keep an average of one in ten. Space, common sense, and mold just don't allow keeping everything! If any of these souvenirs brings back sad or bitter memories, you need to consider whether you wouldn't be better off closing the door on that part of your life and moving on.

Take Pictures

One nice alternative to saving bulky items is to take pictures of the items and let the pictures act as your mementos, rather than saving the space-taking objects themselves. This works well for your old trophies and children's school projects, too. Whether it's a kindergartener's sculpture or your eighth-grader's science project, take a picture of the child with the object at the time it comes home. Then you'll have the picture as your memento long after the object has disappeared.

DIGGING OUT: FINISHING THE JOB

The Arbie Approach to Sorting Out Belongings

Now it's time to actually roll up your sleeves and work at the hardest part of organizing possessions: sorting through individual items and deciding which to keep and which to dispose of. (Remember, the more things you can get rid of, the less you'll have to organize next time around!)

Let's say you've targeted a small entry closet near your front door. Begin somewhere—anywhere, so long as it's one specific place. It could be the clothes on hangers, the floor, or the first shelf. Let's start with the shelf. Remembering the ABCs of accomplishing a task, gather supplies you'll need for this project, including three receptacles, and do your best to make decisions as you sort objects into three categories.

1. Keep
2. Discard
3. Undecided

After you've gone through things once, you'll be "in practice" because you've become accustomed to decision-making. Then go back to your "Undecided" receptacle and you'll find it easier to sort out those items into either "Keep" or "Discard."

The Two-Step Approach

Once you've mastered the "Arbie approach" described above, you may feel confident enough to move on to a somewhat more complex process on your next sorting job. Your preliminary decision will be either to (a) keep it, or (b) get rid of it.

If you want to keep it, a secondary decision is needed. Do you want to (a) store it where it is, or (b) move it to another spot? If it's winter and you use the scarf regularly and that's the handiest place for you to grab it, then you'll want to keep it there, so put it in the "Replace" container. If you use that scarf only occasionally and the closet is overcrowded, you may want to move it someplace else. Place it in the "Move" container.

For major housecleaning tasks, separate belongings into five categories.

(Items placed there will be put away at the end of the sorting session.)

If you want to get rid of the scarf, some secondary decisions are also needed. Do you want to (a) sell it, (b) give it away, or (c) throw it away? Place it in the appropriate box or bag.

Continue making decisions as you come to each item, until you are finished with that shelf.

Clean the shelf and replace the items you still want to keep there. (In fact, anytime you see an empty drawer or shelf—say, when all the glasses are in the dishwasher—utilize that time to wipe off the shelf then, rather than going on a cleaning spree when all the glasses have been put away on the shelf.)

Now check your watch. If you have time to continue, do so, *but be sure to leave enough time to finish putting everything away after you quit the actual sorting.* If time is short, quit and take the throwaways out to your waste receptacles—*now!*—and deliver the other items to appropriate spots.

Take the "Move" items to their new storage places, keeping in mind Stephanie Winston's rules for storage:

- *Keep frequently used items close to their place of use and easily accessible.*
- *Keep infrequently used items in more remote locations and in less accessible places.*

Then you'll be left with only those items you want to give away or sell. Beware! This is where many people get caught. If you can conveniently deliver any of those objects now, do so. Probably, however, you'll have to call a charitable organization to pick up the items, or you may have to take them to a resale shop, or you might want to have a garage sale. Make that decision *right now.* If you can, make the appropriate calls to have the items picked up, or at least schedule your call, garage sale, or other appropriate action on your calendar *right now* so you don't forget to complete your tasks. Otherwise you'll be stuck with this stuff again indefinitely. Do it now!

Cycling

If, after reading this chapter, you still have trouble making decisions, we offer another alternative: Try cycling your unused belongings out.

Let's say you are inclined to keep all of your possessions from babyhood on, even though you never even look at most of them. Allow some leeway for certain beloved items, but put the rest of those items you can't decide on in a covered box in a rough storage area, out of your sight. Don't open that box for several days, but after that, if there's a specific object you need, give yourself permission to resurrect it (but no others). Agree to keep the box for one to three months, then dispose of anything left in it. (Ordinarily you'll never even think of any of those objects again.)

You can also cycle out daily newspapers, magazines, your mate's old painting clothes, or your children's toys (with their permission and involvement).

Make a Regular Schedule

Don't wear yourself out trying to accomplish an enormous task. Unfortunately, the "Arbie way" would be to start reorganizing the whole house or office and not quit until you are totally exhausted. Though that might get the job done, it will burn you out so you'll never want to do it again. Instead, we advise you to pace yourself. Make a regular schedule. To get started, set aside just thirty minutes or an hour every Saturday morning, for instance, or fifteen minutes before you leave for work each Tuesday, or an hour each Wednesday evening. *When* isn't as important as *that it gets done.* When you incorporate getting organized into a regular routine, it becomes very easy to make it a part of your lifestyle, and by starting with small amounts of time, you can gather momentum for larger projects. Remember the slogan, *Success by the yard is hard, but success by the inch is a cinch!*

Daily Maintenance

While we're discussing a regular schedule, we'd like to point out the importance of spending time every day on what we call "daily maintenance." By this we mean *setting aside a specific time each day to put away clutter.* In our own homes and offices, our goal is *to ensure that your surroundings are neat enough to receive unexpected guests without embarrassment.* This not only saves us chagrin, but also helps us avoid wasting time later in trying to find things we need.

This isn't a lofty goal. It's not meant as a deep cleaning time—filing every paper or whisking away the most unobtrusive spiderweb. It's simply a time to clean off your desk at the office (sorting out and straightening papers, files, periodicals, and so on) or tidying up the kitchen in your home and spending no more than five minutes in each of the other rooms (putting away papers, shoes, games, snack residue, and other litter, tossing out trash, and giving the bathroom fixtures a quick swipe to remove obvious spots).

This may seem like inadequate time to you, but if you've followed Don Aslett's admonition that it's easier to *keep* a place clean than it is to *get* it clean, you'll realize that since it was cleaned up only yesterday, it won't take long to rectify it again today. Only long-term accumulations become overwhelming.

SUMMARY

- *Divide and conquer your work by breaking your tasks down into units.*
- *Accomplish tasks by anticipating your needs, not leaving until your task is complete, and doing only what you set out to do.*
- *In deciding what to keep, ask yourself (1) How long since I used this item? (2) Can I justify keeping it? (3) What will happen if it's gone? 4) Is it an irritant?*
- *After deciding what to keep, store it close to where you use it, if you use it often.*
- *For indecision, try "cycling" out your belongings.*
- *Pace yourself.*
- *Set aside a specific time each day to put clutter away.*

10

. . . AND WHERE TO PUT IT

Organize Before Increasing

If you are truly vowing to clean out your home or office, consider space first. People commonly think they don't have enough storage space, and their first inclination is to add more. The first rule of thumb for both paper and possessions, however, is to *organize existing space before adding more.* By weeding out your drawers, files, shelves, and closets, you can utilize existing space more effectively.

Remember, too, that as an Arbie your storage needs may be very different from those of your Elbie counterparts. Elbies are very comfortable—in fact, they *prefer*—to file papers vertically within closed filing cabinets, place their rough storage in covered boxes, hang their clothes vertically on hangers in a closed closet, keep their pens, pencils, paper clips, and other paraphernalia divided into sections in their desk drawers, and so on.

Arbies, on the other hand—and as we've said before—are *visually oriented* and want *direct access,* which results in their having special needs when it comes to storage containers, organizers, or tools. If you're an Arbie, your main need may be to have organizers that provide direct visual view and direct access, without intermediate steps.

And therein lies the problem. Because most organizing tools are created by left-brain people, for left-brain people, filing cabinets, dresser drawers, closets, and other closed apparatus may be unsuitable for your needs because they don't meet the visibility and access criteria.

We have noticed one particular phenomenon that we've jokingly dubbed "the bag-lady syndrome." We have observed that many right-brain-dominant people prefer to store their possessions in open bags. This can be seen while traveling. Elbies neatly fold everything into squarish closed suitcases, while Arbies tend to toss their things into open bags.

> Nichole often travels to conferences with a dear friend, Shirley, and it has gotten to be a joke between them. Betty's clothing is always contained within one or two suitcases, while Shirley's items are separated into many little bags. She'll put cosmetics in one, clothes in another, lingerie in yet another, and so forth. Betty once quietly joked to a bellhop about all of Shirley's little bags, but the bellhop didn't see anything unusual about it, and matter-of-factly responded that many people travel that way.

Since we heard the above story, we've become aware of this phenomenon, and now understand the reason for the growing market for every size and type of utility bag sold in innumerable stores.

Organizers

There are infinite numbers of organizers on the market, made to hold everything from cosmetics to carpentry tools, and we heartily endorse buying or making organizers you can use. Beware, however, of buying organizers in a store where they look appealing to you, and trying to figure out what to do with them when you bring them back to your home or office! Shop carefully, and always know ahead of time exactly where you're going to put an organizer and that it will fit where you want to put it. Also, be sure of what you're going to put in it, and that it will be natural for you to use. Otherwise you may just be adding to your clutter!

The One-Step Advantage

The let-it-all-hang-out type of storage appeals to an Arbie's visual orientation (which, as we want to stress again, is not inferior to, but merely *different from,* that of the Elbie), along with the need for uncomplicated direct access to whatever is wanted. Although the simple process of opening a closet door or dresser drawer doesn't seem like much of a hurdle to Elbies, when it comes to putting things away, just one little extra step in the process can dissuade Arbies from doing it.

Also, when trying to find things, having to search "behind closed doors" can be taxing—especially if the objects inside aren't sorted according to type. If lingerie, jewelry, scarves, and hose are indiscriminately mixed together within several drawers, for instance, finding the exact item wanted may prove to be difficult. Of course, open storage can quickly become messy looking, so you may want to consider your needs—and the needs of others—before deciding what's best for you. If others object, you could perhaps keep your things in an adjoining room, or merely cover up your open storage when necessary by keeping an afghan handy to conceal it.

Departments

Think of getting away from tradition and creating "departments" by putting things together that you use at the same time. For example, if you often make yourself a cup of instant coffee, rather than having to run all over the kitchen to collect your spoon, cup, coffee, water, sugar, and so on, store your coffee, measuring spoon, and sugar together with your coffee mugs on a shelf between the water supply and your coffeemaker. With everything at your fingertips, you've simplified the entire coffeemaking process by creating a "coffee department."

Consider the following possibilities:

- A "dressing department," where everything you need for getting ready to go to work is within easy reach.
- A "copy department" at your office, with copier supplies and equipment, including glass-cleaning solution and paper towels, all stored next to the copier for quick and easy use, together with scissors, hole punch, stapler, and so on.

A "coffee department" is one example of how you can cluster items that you use together.

- A "gift-wrapping department" that holds wrapping paper, ribbon, scissors, and tape. If you mail gifts often, you could add boxes, strong tape, labels, and so forth. If you send them via a delivery company, keep the forms you'll need to fill out with your wrappings, so that everything is together and easily found when needed.

Other "departments" might include a "baking department," a "hobby department," or a "research department."

Exposed Wall Space

If you're short on storage space, take a good look around and consider possibilities you might have overlooked. *Any exposed wall, floor, ceiling, or hollow or open space represents a potential storage space.*

Look to blank walls where

- shelving might be built
- enclosed furniture might be added (e.g., wardrobes)

Look at open floor space, where you might

- build freestanding shelving,
- center desks or filing cabinets
- install an "island" of back-to-back furniture

Look at the tops of furniture, where

- storage boxes could be put in a rough storage area
- individual items could be displayed

Look at ceilings or upper walls, from which

- tension wires might be strung to display hanging objects
- pegboard and/or hooks might be installed to hang things
- holders might be built to suspend items (for instance, skis against rafters or cradles for extra lumber)

Look at open space in storage areas, where you can

- extend shelving in closets or cupboards
- install extra shelves between existing ones
- hang items to fill the center open space (see the suggestions above for utilizing ceilings and upper walls)

Look for hollow spaces

- to recess storage between studs in the walls (make sure that no wiring, vents, etc., are in your way)

- to recess storage between rafters in the ceiling
- under beds or skirted sofas
- inside unused suitcases
- behind doors

Be creative! The possibilities are endless.

Vertical Storage

Another storage guideline is very simple: Store long, flat items in long, flat places! Look around your home or office for long items lying flat, and find a place to store them on end to take the least floor or base space.

- Store elongated items—barbecue equipment, paintbrushes, scissors, cosmetics, pencils, etc.—upright in a holder. Look

Stand long, narrow items on end for storage; papers can be stored vertically, too.

around for unused items that might serve as attractive holders (planters, vases, mugs).

- Stand flags, poles, or other larger elongated items on end in corners or the ends of closets.
- File papers, magazines, maps, brochures, catalogs, etc., vertically.

If you think horizontally, as many Arbies do, you'll need to figure out what works best for you.

Create Natural Places

When you're creating storage places for your different "departments" of belongings, do your best to create a place for each item that is convenient, natural, and *easy for you to use.*

If it seems as though extra effort will be required to put something away, you may find yourself leaving it out and making excuses instead. If a box of new file folders is buried at the bottom of a supply cabinet, for instance, you may not replace the box where it belongs.

In your office, if your filing drawer is in a remote location you may find yourself making excuses rather than returning an item to its rightful home. This is also true of children's possessions, shop tools, games, or anything else. The solution to these dilemmas is to arrange your storage so that it's natural for you to use and everything is easy to get in and out.

Step Shelves

A "step shelf" is an extra shelf placed on an existing surface to double the storage there. These extra shelves often cover only a part of an existing shelf, and they can come in many forms. They can be homemade by supporting a board on two tin cans (the old brick-and-board bookshelf idea); or they can be purchased at housewares or office-supply departments anywhere. Ready-made ones are often constructed of vinyl over metal, the same as a dish drainer or the shelves of a dishwasher.

Step shelves can be utilized wherever there's enough open space within shelving. For example, if such things as canned goods or stationery boxes take up six vertical inches of a shelf, and another eight inches are open above that, storage space can be doubled by placing a step shelf over the existing items to hold another set of cans or supplies.

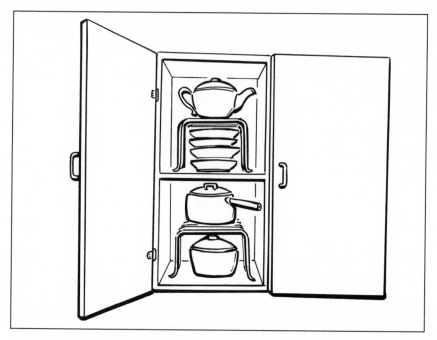

Step-shelves can double your storage space in some cupboards.

BEDROOMS AND CLOSETS

The Ideal Arbie Bedroom

If you're an Arbie, your ideal bedroom might not even contain a closet or dressers. (A lot of the ones you have now may be filled up with the stuff you never use anyway.) Instead, in this imaginary bedroom, one wall might have a row of doorknobs to hang clothes, with chairs under them. Jackets could be hung across the chair backs. Shoes could go underneath. Instead of dressers with drawers, another wall could support flat surfaces on which to put things such as loose change, wallets, glasses, and other miscellaneous stuff. A third wall would be covered with large, open cubbyholes so you could quickly stash

The Arbie's ideal bedroom would probably have no closets at all—just plenty of doorknobs and chairs to hang clothes on.

items such as jewelry, belts, scarves, and other items that needed a home.

Few Arbies would feel comfortable admitting they would maintain a bedroom like that—believing it to be socially unacceptable. *Many Arbies, however, have candidly admitted to us that if no one else ever had to see the bedroom, they'd love it—and actually find it more convenient to use!*

Closets and Clothing

Just in case you really do like and use your closet and want to utilize it as effectively as possible, here are some guidelines that may help:

If you are handy or can afford to have your closet remodeled by a closet company, we highly recommend removing the standard shelf running across the length of a single hanger rod and installing double rods, drawers, and/or sets of vertical shelving.

If you're creative, you may enjoy designing your space to

meet your own unique needs. Since this is sort of a science all its own, we won't get into designing details, except to suggest that you utilize wall storage space all the way to the ceiling and store everything off the floor to make cleaning easier.

Clothes on Hangers

For clothes on hangers, however, we do have several suggestions—especially if you're short of space.

First, remove all the empty hangers and retain only a reasonable number of them together at one end of the rod (or elsewhere, if you prefer). This may free up more space than you had imagined possible.

Next, remove everything you don't wear currently, following the recommendations found earlier in this chapter. Store out-of-season clothes in empty suitcases, boxes, bags, or covered hanger bags in another closet or in a dry area of your basement or attic—but make sure such areas are moth- and mildew-proof.

Now you're ready to reorganize what's left. Just put all your jackets together in one section, and put your shirts, shorts, trousers, and so forth together to form other sections.

You may suddenly begin to appreciate how many pairs of brown pants, navy sport coats, or green skirts you have. It will definitely help you plan your wardrobe better, allowing you to see what you do or don't have.

Perhaps a happy medium, somewhere between this approach and the Ideal Arbie Bedroom described earlier, would work for you.

At this point you may be feeling overwhelmed with the innumerable details discussed in the last two chapters. If that is the case, we suggest you skip ahead to Chapter 13 to read about inner struggles that individuals experience in trying to get organized. After switching to a more right-brain concept for a while, you may be more ready to return to Chapters 11 and 12, which discuss papers and periodicals and how to keep track of them.

SUMMARY

- *Organize your existing storage spaces before adding more.*
- *Buy "user friendly" organizers.*
- *Create "departments" by storing like things together.*
- *Any exposed wall, floor, ceiling, or hollow or open space represents a potential storage space.*
- *Even though you may naturally think horizontally, watch for vertical storage opportunities.*
- *Step shelves can double storage space.*
- *The bedroom may be the most striking example of differences of organizing styles. Create whatever is acceptable to you (and your mate).*

11

PAPER PARADISE!

Whether you're a homemaker or a business owner, managing your paper is likely to be your biggest single organizing challenge. The sheer volume of paper that modern life seems to generate makes it difficult for almost everyone. We have learned over the years, however, that certain people, including many who exhibit left-brain skills in other areas, have trouble managing paper because they don't feel comfortable utilizing standard filing systems. In the next two chapters we'll offer some effective suggestions for getting from Paper Hell to Paper Paradise—including some traditional methods and some unorthodox paper-managing styles that have worked for the Arbies we have counseled or taught.

In this chapter we'll discuss the organizing styles of two very different kinds of people. Then we will give you specific techniques—depending on your style—for "digging out" from under an accumulation of paper and periodicals. Finally, we'll discuss paper management—with methods for maintaining order on an ongoing basis.

DIFFERENT ORGANIZING STYLES

As you read the following descriptions, you'll doubtless decide you fall somewhere between Linda's and Ryan's extreme organizing styles—identifying with Linda in some respects and with Ryan in others:

Linda's Style

Linda is an Elbie perfectionist whose office is always neat and tidy. There is never excess paper on Linda's desk. Her calendar book holds careful notes of every detail of her life. Her desk drawers are in perfect order, with a place for everything and everything in its place. Her file drawers are in perfect order, her filing is always up to date, and she is secure in the knowledge that she can magically retrieve any paper she wants from her files at a moment's notice.

Ryan's Style

Ryan moved into the office next to Linda's over a year ago, with several four-drawer filing cabinets, a computer terminal, a desk, a credenza, and bookshelves—everything one could ever want to stay organized. There was only one hole in his great plans: the standard tools that he chose to maintain order were unnatural for him to use.

Ironically, even though Ryan has a complete complement of furniture and organizing tools at his disposal, he prefers to roll his chair around to an open space and surround himself with a semicircle of stacks of papers on his office floor. (One of the reasons he does this, of course, is that his desk is already covered with an assortment of papers, periodicals, folders, and other paraphernalia too numerous to mention).

At income-tax time, he sorted contributions into one pile on the floor, business expenses into another, property taxes into another, and so on. When working on financial papers, he stacked envelopes of bank statements into one pile on the floor, bills to pay next to that, and insurance papers in another stack. He plans to put them all away soon, but he gets "too busy to do it now," and—after he has stepped over them repeatedly—the piles have begun to slide into one another and become indistinguishable.

Now, after a year in his office, every desk drawer is full of papers and miscellaneous paraphernalia, and disarrayed stacks are piled high on top of his credenza, desk, and computer area, as well as on the floor. He has dumped his original files into the file drawers with the promise that he'll purge and reorganize them later—but "later" has never come. Finding papers he needs, *when* he needs them, has become difficult—and sometimes impossible. He is starting to spend hours every week looking for papers he can't find.

There are many dynamics operating in Linda's and Ryan's styles that make them so different.

1. Involvement with the Printed Word. It's easy for Ryan to get involved with the printed word—*really* involved! Whether he picks up *The Wall Street Journal* or *Business Week,* for instance, he is immediately drawn into what he reads, becoming totally absorbed in it. People who love the printed word tend to surround themselves with it. They depend on reading material, remember it, think about what they've read, and feel a relationship to it. And soon they have piles of paper in every available space. Because of this tendency, it's difficult for Ryan to clean off his desk. Rather than swiftly dispatching the material into its proper places, he is drawn into almost every item he picks up. It's much easier for an unemotional Elbie like Linda, or an outsider, to handle papers or possessions effectively because they are not *involved* with their papers.

> *If you tend to be emotionally attached to your papers and periodicals, pay yourself one dollar for every one you discard and use the money to buy yourself a treat. Or find someone who is not a "saver" to help you sort through and dispose of what you don't need.*

2. Seeing Is Remembering. Ryan likes to be able to see every reminder of things he needs to do. It makes him secure to know where everything is, and he feels that if a task is in view he will remember to do it. To him, the saying "Seeing is believing" translates into "Seeing is remembering." Being able to see what he needs to do gives him a feeling of control.

The visually oriented Arbie is reluctant to file papers away out of sight because of a fear of not being able to find them again. The Arbie wants direct access to his or her belongings, without having to go through several steps to find a given object. These are some of the basic reasons why Arbies tend to collect piles of papers on their desks.

Arbies think not only horizontally but also in curved lines rather than straight or squared ones. This is why Ryan—and many other Arbies—tend to arrange piles of papers into a semicircle around them on the floor, rather than sorting their papers into files or even into squared-off stacks on their desks.

3. Global Versus Detail. If Linda decided her office needed cleaning, she might focus on her desk and estimate it would take twenty minutes to clean it. She would then methodically proceed to accomplish that task. But Ryan sees the whole picture—the entire office, including the desk, the credenza, the files, and all of the papers and other stuff strewn about. This immediately becomes overwhelming to him, and paralyzes him into inaction.

If he does begin to get organized, since his natural organizing style is to do things on a global scale, he attempts to accomplish the whole task at once. He begins working "all over the place." He'll pick up one paper from a pile on the credenza and lay it on the table, take a magazine from a table and put it in a file, deliver a memo to the next office, and so forth, without a plan of action.

If you tend to be like Ryan, imagine using a video camera, zooming in on one particular small area and focusing on that. Take a deep breath and relax, ridding yourself of panic. Forget the whole big, unbroken image of your task at hand and forgive yourself for not working on it all at once. Stay focused on that one small area.

If you only manage to deal with three or four papers, that's progress. Don't chastise yourself for not doing more, for not accomplishing the entire overwhelming task. Work at it a little at a time. Quit when you have accomplished what you can handle, but come back to it regularly. Treat yourself to a small reward each time you do this successfully. As you overcome your fear of the overwhelming nature of your task, you'll be able to relax and accomplish more. It is probably more your mental fear of the task than the physical doing of it that is holding you back.

VISUALIZING

Before beginning to straighten out your papers, it would be helpful to take just a few minutes to imagine how your office will look after it's cleaned up. Picture the beautiful woodwork gleaming on the top of your desk. Imagine how neat the insides of your file drawers will look, how great you will feel with your reading material attractively arranged and awaiting your serene attention. Think of how successful you'll feel, reaching into your top drawer and finding the item you need at your fingertips. Visualize how proud you'll feel when the boss or your best friend stops by and compliments you on how neat your office looks.

Once you've vividly imagined how great your office will look, how wonderful you'll feel, how sweet it will smell, you are then ready to move on to the next step.

Phase One: Sorting

Rolling Up Your Sleeves and Doing It

It doesn't really matter where you start your organizing. Here are some considerations, however.

If all of your filing and storage spaces are full, you will need to start there in order to clear out space to make room for other things you want to keep there. Or simply start with the papers in front of you, sort them, move to the stack on your right, handle that, and circle on around your desk until your desktop is clean. Then move to the next piece of furniture on your right, and so on.

Or try tackling your greatest irritant first. Perhaps that would be the upper left-hand shelf of your credenza, where things fall out every time you open the door.

Which place you begin is not so important as starting with one single place and, like a video camera lens, focusing on that only.

After first visualizing and then choosing a starting point, begin rough sorting. This should be done on a regular basis in small segments of time that are set aside specifically for the purpose of sorting and putting away. It can be a set amount of time, such as fifteen minutes, or a designated amount of work to achieve. For instance, you may decide to work until one pile of papers by the telephone is sorted and put away. Include time for preparation and time to put away what you've sorted. Otherwise, you'll only find yourself in a bigger mess. Plan to spend about half of your session sorting, and use the second half for distributing the sorted papers to wherever they belong.

Leave time to finish sorting

Start organizing papers by rough sorting. Designate a certain length of time you'll work—perhaps twenty minutes—then spend ten minutes sorting and ten minutes putting away what you've sorted.

Whether you designate a time frame or an amount of work, *you should not sort for more than one hour.* Otherwise you'll burn yourself out and never want to face the task again. That would be counterproductive because the whole idea is to work on it a little at a time until the whole task is complete.

Pick a specific time when you can work on it every day, or three days a week, or even once a week—say at ten-thirty every Saturday morning—until you are caught up. These specific dates and times need to be scheduled and their priority must be retained at a level as high as any other important appointment on your calendar.

Absolutely *not allowed* during your sorting time should be talking (making phone calls, speaking with a co-worker, etc.); reading (more than just a glance to ascertain the category of each paper); watching TV; listening to the radio; getting a drink; going to the restroom; or any other activity, *including taking action on anything.* If this is achievable only between 3:00 and 4:00 A.M., then so be it. It is imperative, however, that these rules be followed.

Using the examples given previously, Linda "knows" there is only one "right" way to sort or file papers, and that is vertically. She would carefully sort all the papers to be filed according to which file drawer they go into, then methodically file them drawer by drawer. To be effective, she must have every paper filed away in its proper place, and she would be horrified at the idea of using cardboard sorter boxes to stack her papers.

Ryan will probably want to handle his stuff differently (which, again, is not "wrong," but simply in a different manner). He might find that sorter boxes would work like magic for him.

Multi-compartment Sorting Boxes

Stephanie called us two months after her husband had died and said she was feeling depressed. Not only was she grieving the loss of her loved one, but she was also feeling overwhelmed with the responsibility of all the paperwork she now had to handle.

When we arrived, neat stacks of papers almost covered her large dining room table. These had been sorted into a fairly good semblance of order, with bills in one stack, investments in another, and so forth. Still, she was feeling swamped.

We had brought along an eight-compartment desktop literature sorter, and placed it in the middle of the table. We designated the upper right-hand slot for current bills to be paid, and as we sorted, every item we found that fell into that category was placed in that space. She had a number of items for her grown children, so those papers were placed in the slot under the bills. Below that, we slid in bank statements. Since it was February, federal 1040 forms regarding the previous year's investments were arriving, so all tax papers for the previous year were placed together in the bottom right section.

More papers were categorized and divided into the four left-hand sections as well. In one hour's time, our widowed client's transition was incredible. The furrows of her brow began to relax, and in the end she was smiling with newfound confidence. What had been an overwhelming-looking blanket covering her entire dining room table had suddenly become an organized, visible condensation of papers. She could now reach any paper she wanted to find without feeling that they were hidden away in a huge block of vertical files, yet they weren't covering every square inch of working space. Best of all, they were stored horizontally, something very important to the right-brain-dominant person.

Multi-compartment desktop sorters are a nice alternative to filing cabinets—and are certainly better than boxes or piles! They can be purchased at office-supply stores, but the nine-compartment cardboard shoe organizers sold in housewares departments often work just as well. (The sections of shoe holders are made in slightly different sizes, so be sure the ones you select are big enough to accommodate 8-inch-wide papers.) True literature sorters can be purchased that are made of inexpensive cardboard, hard plastic, or wood (though these are more expensive). These sorters can be used temporarily just for sorting papers and then removed to a holding place, or maintained permanently as a horizontal "hot file" to hold currently active papers. Labels (especially color-coded ones) for each compartment are helpful, but because of the papers' visibility, they aren't an absolute necessity.

These sorters would appeal to Ryan for the very reasons they would be rejected by Linda. They are casual, not formal. They are plain, not elegant; horizontal, not vertical; out in the open, not hidden. Best of all, they are easy to use.

Instead of giving the overall impression of unending piles of work to do, the sorter allows a feeling of control—that the papers can be reached at a finger's touch, yet don't have to be spread out to form an overwhelming-looking burden of re-

Multi-compartment sorters are simple to use, but they can help you do away with a lot of clutter.

sponsibility. Certainly it is much better than having no organizing system at all. Ryan, for instance, knows he wants to keep his income tax papers in the "nine-holer" in the back corner of his office, the project he's currently working on in a compartment right by his desk, and the instructions for his new laser printer in the unit by his computer. Even without labeling, he knows he'll be able to see those thick blue instructions easily the next time he needs them. As his needs expand, he will add more units. A new multicompartment box provides empty spaces that need to be filled. Ryan enjoys utilizing this opportunity and soon will have every hole stuffed with his papers.

Other storage methods that work well for Ryan are loose-leaf ring binders and "pocket" folders. He likes them because he can buy them in attractive colors and in interesting sizes that correspond to his needs.

He establishes a slim green binder with pocket pages to collect prices on an investment he's about to make, an attractive burgundy-colored binder to hold transparencies and information about a seminar he's developing, and—the best one of all—a bright red binder with plastic protector sheets to hold numerous lists of telephone numbers, account references, and other lists he refers to regularly. These lists used to be scattered across his desk, taped to the side of his computer, and tacked on the wall beside his desk. Now he has a convenient place for all of them. These three binders have now expanded into eight, all neatly arranged on a bookshelf within easy reach of his desk.

Step 1. Sorting Papers into Categories

Before you start sorting, take a couple of minutes to visualize once again how you will accomplish the task, how much nicer things will look, and *how good you'll feel*—in just thirty minutes or an hour. Designate a certain amount of work you're going to do during this particular session. Then make your dreams come true.

Designate three places and a wastebasket to divide your papers into. These places can be piles on your desk (if there is enough room for them), or boxes, crates, or whatever you wish.

Start by rough-sorting your papers into two categories:

- Keep
- Toss

If you're going to dispose of it, pitch it into the wastebasket now. *Remember, you'll never again even think of most of the things you throw away.*

If you're going to keep it, rough-sort it into one of the following categories:

- Reading
- Storage/filing
- Action/decisions

(If other materials are mixed in with your papers—from fishing equipment to pictures to promotional buttons—throw away as many as you can as you come to them, and provide a fourth place to hold the rest.)

Step 2. Handling the Papers You've Sorted

Reading. The "Reading" materials can quickly be moved to wherever you do your reading. Linda would stand these materials neatly on a bookshelf, table, basket, folder, or other place nearby. Ryan's inclination would be to just leave the box on the floor by his reading chair.

Make up a "Reading" folder to hold single pages, and include it with your other reading materials. Tear out articles you want to peruse, and place those in the folder too. Perhaps you want to create an attractive reading box or basket if you don't already have one. But beware: *Do not stop and read anything right now—or spend time creating that attractive place!* Just deposit your reading there and move on to the next item.

Storage/filing. Only two categories left! Hey, this is easy!

Sort papers and reading material into four categories.

This is the category for any papers that must be kept for reference later. *Take the time right now to do your filing*—in a filing cabinet or by using another method for paper storage. To Linda, this naturally means vertically filing in file drawers, but it doesn't necessarily mean the same thing to Ryan. (At this point we only want to encourage you to actually handle them now. Where and how to go about doing this will be described later in this chapter.)

Action/decisions. Your organizing session is almost complete! Sort "action" papers into three groups:

• *"Hot"/Important.* These are items that require immediate attention. As you're sorting, *don't act on anything right then!* If you run across something that is far overdue and demands immediate attention, remind yourself that it's waited this long and it can wait another fifteen minutes

Leave reading material next to your favorite chair—but don't sit down yet!

until you finish your sorting and distributing and filing. *Only then should you take action on that item.*

- *Routine.* These are papers that need action after the "hot" items are handled. Included within your Routine Action can be items to be delegated to others. If these need to be physically delivered (perhaps to others' offices) collect these together and deliver them all in one trip when your sorting is done.

- *Decisions to make.* Now that you're in a decision-making mode, you can tackle this group with more confidence. Make your best guess as to where to go with these papers.

Your sorting period is finished. Now—*and only now*—it's time to begin working on your most important action items.

Phase Two: Filing/Storing Your Papers

Create places ready to catch every type of paper. In a corporate setting, filing must be formal and uniform. Personal storage, however, can be set up the way you can most easily retrieve your papers.

The Elbie characteristically labels empty spaces and subsequently files items under the "proper" headings. For the Arbie, the other way around works best. In other words, Arbies find it more comfortable to start with an empty nine-compartment box that has no sections labeled. As piles of somewhat related papers accumulate, he or she then simply puts those papers into a section of the nine-holer. It is handy, though, to have a sheet of paper listing the nine categories, especially if you require several nine-holers to get the job done.

The Home Front

For the home, we recommend storing your personal papers in two broad categories: *personal* and *financial.* The following are suggested files or cubbyholes you may want to create for yourself:

Personal papers.
- *Action items.* These could include to-do's, classes you may attend, correspondence to answer, sales to attend, invitations, appointments, schedules, pending/follow-up and/or miscellaneous projects.
- *Items for others to see.*
- *Copies to make.*
- *Warranties and instructions.*
- *Resources/Reference.* Almost everyone collects information about their areas of interest—woodworking, gardening, sports, investments, health, religion, or whatever. These can be stored under the broad category of Resources or Reference, whichever appeals to you, and then divided

into folders according to topics. *Caution: Don't over-collect. Keep only a reasonable amount of information.*
• *Numerous other categories.*

Financial information. Financial papers need to be kept separate from other personal papers. We suggest that the following file folders or sorter compartments be established:

• *Bills to be paid/Financial follow-up.* Included in this category could also be anything else you need to write checks for, such as catalog orders and charitable contributions.
• *Receipts.* Once bills are paid, the remainder of the statements and receipts you want to keep can be stored for income tax records or other purposes. These receipts can be divided into categories such as Automobile, Banking, Contributions, Credit Cards, etc. Preprinted manila accordion "home files," available at office-supply stores, are handy for this, and will fit right into a standard filing cabinet drawer. Empty the home file at the year's end by putting each category of receipt into separate envelopes and holding them in a box for tax purposes. The home file can then be reused the following year.
• *Important papers.* Deeds, wills, insurance policies, birth and marriage certificates, and other important papers should be kept in safe-deposit boxes at a bank or vault company, or in a fireproof safe at home.
• *Other categories.* Separate slots or folders should be kept for papers on cars, real estate, insurance, and so forth.

Please note that for personal file folders, *labeling your files is important,* but the formality or propriety of the name you use is absolutely unimportant. The essential thing is that the name should make sense to you, the user. For instance, the place you keep your bills to be paid can be called "Checks to Write," "Bills to Pay," "Financial Follow-up," "Expenses," or simply "$." This requires consideration on your part, because if the name of this category doesn't make the appropriate mental connection or carries a negative connotation, you won't be as likely to utilize it properly. "Items for Others to See" could bear others' names or titles ("Spouse," "Children," etc.). This folder could also hold mail for others to see and be called "Today's Mail."

One businesswoman reported that she kept only one file in her attaché case, and it was reserved exclusively for a few key papers that absolutely demanded action that day. She labeled that file "Today, Dammit!" It worked for her.

As you sort papers, you will doubtless become aware of some papers that seem to go together—insurance papers, for instance—but that don't seem to have a "home." When that happens, establish a place for them. Either make a folder with an appropriate label, a new compartment in your sorter, or a divided space within a loose-leaf binder.

At the Office

Think of broad general categories first when setting up your filing—whether in a vertical system, binders, or horizontal nine-holers. One of the pitfalls your authors have noted repeatedly in business office filing systems is the lack of these general headings in large filing systems. As an example, folders for associations will typically be filed under the name of the association, e.g., the National Association of XYZ will be filed under *N*; the American Association of XYZ will be filed under *A*; and the XYZ Association of America will be filed under *X*.

The most effective way to set up your files is to use general categories, with subheadings behind those. Consider, for instance, setting up main headings for "Associations" (or "Organizations") and then alphabetically filing the different association folders as subheadings behind the main category.

As another example, if you have clients located in different Ohio cities, rather than filing each folder under the separate clients' names, a main category could be created under *C,* for "Clients," with subheadings behind that of "Akron," "Columbus," and "Dayton," for instance, with appropriate clients filed alphabetically behind each city subheading.

A cautionary note: Never make a folder, a slot, or a binder division for less than five to ten papers. If there are only a few sheets, combine them into a category with other papers. Car insurance papers might fit better into a file of other insurance papers than in a file of their own. Rather that making a separate space for the list of members in an organization you belong to, combine that list with other lists you want to refer to frequently.

Paper Clips

A word about the lowly but invaluable paper clip. Paper clips are notorious for scooping up extra unwanted papers on the bottom or back side of other papers they are holding together. Always check to make sure you haven't inadvertently picked up unwanted papers on the back of a group you're working on. Since many clips tend to make stacks of paper lopsided, staple papers together whenever possible. Make it a firm rule to remove clips and to staple papers together when filing. Since this requires extra attention to detail, you'll have to force yourself to do it. It's well worth the short time it takes, however, because it can save untold hours of looking for lost items that have unintentionally been clipped to the backs of other papers.

PHASE THREE: ONGOING PAPER MANAGEMENT

Once you've succeeded in "digging out," and have established natural places to hold your papers, it's time to begin maintaining the order you've established. Be especially aware of accepting any new papers you create or that are given to you. Realize that every time you write a note to yourself, you have created yet another piece of paper for which you now have responsibility. Become more judicious about creating papers—in the form of reminder notes to yourself, copies of memos or letters you write to others, notes taken at meetings, and so on.

Also, become more discerning about accepting papers from others. Just because something came in the mail addressed to you doesn't mean you are required to keep it. When papers are passed out at meetings, or when you have opportunities to pick up literature on real estate, travel, or anything else that might interest you, *think twice before you take one;* remember that you will have to figure out what to do with it.

To the Arbie, almost anything takes precedence over cleaning and straightening and filing; putting things away is not only unimportant, but spending time doing so seems to be a complete waste of time. This causes an internal dilemma because the person is simultaneously pulled in opposite directions: on the one hand, he knows that restoring order would be beneficial, but at the same time, thoughts about other things he wants to do lure him away from cleaning up. Your success in keeping your papers organized depends upon two things: your daily habits, and religiously scheduling regular sorting and filing sessions on an ongoing basis.

If you are convinced that order would make your life simpler and less stressful in the long run, then you will spend an adequate amount of time seeing that things are put away in the short run. It's as simple as that, because *the neatness of any space is in direct proportion to the amount of effort spent keeping it that way.*

Follow Each Action with a Reaction

Each time you do almost anything, that action requires some sort of tool or object to carry it out. At your desk, this means letters, file folders, periodicals, and computer printouts, along with pens, staple pullers, and other paraphernalia.

Make it a habit to put away whatever you were using immediately after you are finished with it. We know this may be difficult for you, but do the best you can to "follow each action with a reaction." Unless you react by cleaning up every time you act, you'll end up with layers of papers on your desk by the day's end. If you put things away as you use them, very little will be left to clean up at quitting time.

Keep Distractions Out of the Way

You might want to learn to keep items you aren't currently working on out of direct view. If you are visually oriented, it's all too easy to become distracted when everything is out in plain sight. You would do well to put items not being used at the moment behind you, perhaps on a credenza, so that you can concentrate only on what you're working on at the moment. Taking a few moments to find an appropriate holding place for every type of paper that arrives at your desk will pay dividends in the long run.

Set Aside a Specific Daily Maintenance Time

The other necessity for retaining order is to religiously spend a certain amount of time doing daily maintenance. We suggest you do that at the time when you're at your best—your most alert and productive time of day. If you're a "morning person," set aside fifteen minutes at a certain time every morning to "clean up." If you're more alert later in the day, do it then. *When* isn't so important as *that* you do it every day.

Besides your regular maintenance time, we suggest you begin cleaning up your desk sooner than usual at day's end. If you normally leave your desk at 5:00 P.M. each day and usually spend only five minutes piling your papers into stacks or stuffing them into drawers before you go, then we suggest you mentally tell yourself you are leaving at 4:45 P.M. each day instead, and start putting and filing things away then. This may seem wasteful to you, because you may be concerned that you'll be "quitting" fifteen minutes early. But if this fifteen minutes translates into thirty or forty-five minutes you would otherwise spend looking for papers the next day, you'll actually be *saving* fifteen to thirty minutes per day. This won't be wasted time at all, but rather a different kind of productive time. Remember, "a stitch in time saves nine."

If you work for a person who might raise his or her eyebrows at the appearance of your "packing up" early at the end of your workday, to alleviate suspicions ahead of time it might be a good idea to explain to that person that from now on you will be utilizing that time to do your filing and daily maintenance. Then be sure you do it!

Mail Handling

When you receive your mail, resist the temptation to open only those envelopes that interest you and leave the rest. With good intentions, too many people think they'll deal with the rest "later"—which means piles of junk mail accumulate. Instead, delay opening *any* of your mail until you have time to deal with it properly. Set aside a specific time at a certain hour each day to handle your mail completely.

Envelopes

Do not maintain your papers in envelopes, but rather *throw away all envelopes immediately.* If you need the return address from an envelope, make a note of it right away and then throw out the envelope. Envelopes take extra space, tend to be ragged, and obscure what's inside. They make poor holders for papers (with a few possible exceptions, such as bank statements or other small items that need to be held together). Don't use them for lists or notes, either; you can afford appropriate notepads. Again *throw envelopes away.* Period.

Calendar Notations

Make calendar notations as you open your mail. Write down not only appointment dates and times, but any other information you may need at that time. Perhaps you'll need the address or phone number (either for a last-minute confirmation or for a baby-sitter), directions to get there, or a list of items you'll need to remember to take. This can be an invaluable aid when you are hurriedly trying to leave.

Touch It Once

As you sort existing piles of papers or handle incoming mail, make it a goal to handle each paper only once. This is an idealistic concept that isn't always feasible, but work toward that goal to the extent possible. Anything that is true junk, of course, should be pitched immediately, handling it only one time. Ask yourself, "Do I (or anyone I live or work with) care?" If not, throw it out now. Be sure a wastebasket is always available right where you work, because if any kind of trip is involved to throw papers away, you will be tempted to lay the item down with the promise that you'll "throw it away later"—thus creating a pile that will need to be handled again.

As you sort or open mail, touch it once and put every paper right where it goes. If it's to be filed, put it in a filing box, folder, or pile. If it's reading, put it in a designated reading spot; if it needs action, put it in your "action" holder.

It's important, however, not to shuffle paper from one place to the next. That's when you begin getting into trouble. Every time you pick up a paper, look at it, and put it back down to work on something else, you are handling that paper again—and sometimes again—and again. . . .

The Measles

A well-known technique can help you become aware of how many times you've handled the same paper. Each time you handle a paper, use a red pencil to place a small red dot in the upper right corner. When the same paper has accumulated so many dots it looks as though it has measles, you will realize how often you have handled it.

If you find yourself handling the same papers repeatedly, ask yourself, "What do I need to get this job done?" Sometimes it will require a decision. Perhaps it's an invitation to an event you haven't decided about attending. Other papers may, for example, require a phone call to collect information. When you have figured out what it will take to handle that paper, make a written note on your calendar or to-do list for the appropriate time to handle that task. Then place the paper where you can find it—and where you won't rehandle it repeatedly before it's finally completed—perhaps in a "Pending" folder, "hot" file, or cubbyhole.

In Today, Out Today

To the greatest extent possible, live by the "in today, out today" rule. If you return phone calls, answer your correspondence, deal with customer complaints, record expenses, and so forth on the day they happen, you will never run behind.

Looking for Things You Can't Find

People like Ryan often have a tough time finding things. Being unable to find lost items, in fact, becomes a frustration for them on a regular basis. In this case, Ryan attended an especially interesting insurance seminar a few months ago, and now wants to refer to his notes concerning a liability issue he is discussing with his client. But alas!—he can't find them!

Let's take a look at some of the reasons this may happen. *Ryan's mind is involved with other thoughts.* Instead of concentrating on his search, his mind may be enmeshed in other current activities—rehashing last night's argument with his teenage son, or rehearsing what he'll say to the difficult client at his three o'clock appointment today.

His mind gets so absorbed in these other interests that he is reluctant to pay attention to the mundane. That was what was happening when he laid down his notes in the first place, and that is what happens again when he tries to retrieve them.

Once something is lost, it can be difficult for Ryan to become focused on looking for a specific item because *he is experiencing "inner noise"*—agitation within himself from a variety of sources. These might include anger at himself for losing the notes, impatience to get off to where he's going, frustration that once again he has lost something, and so on. At this point he may become panicky, and fear and anxiety may prevent him from seeing the notes when they are right in front of him.

Besides his inability to focus on the search, *he may also be doing a lot of self-deprecation* as he looks. "I'm so stupid!" he tells himself. "Why can't I ever learn?" It's difficult for Ryan to concentrate on anything else when his thoughts are fully consumed with his own failures.

Not expecting to find something is a reason in itself for not being able to find it. Once Ryan convinces himself he is incapable of "ever finding anything," he mentally quits looking. By putting himself down, he experiences a loss of confidence in his ability to find anything. This self-destructive attitude then becomes prophetic, and indeed he can't find what he needs.

Still another reason Ryan has trouble locating what he wants is *an incorrect but vivid visual image of how the item looks.* He may think the seminar notes were taken on a standard yellow tablet, when in fact they were written on smaller white notepaper. The item may be directly before his eyes a dozen times while he ransacks his office looking for his notes, but he can't "see" them because they look different from his preconceived idea of their appearance.

If you identify with any of the above, the next time you are looking for something you can't find, stop! Take a minute to think very carefully. Calm yourself down and realize you are not stupid for having lost something. You are a creative person whose thoughts were absorbed elsewhere when you put the item down in the first place. Now you need to tell yourself you are perfectly able to find it again.

Think back to the last time you used the item, and try to retrace your steps from that point. If you went to the next room, did you look in there? Could something have been laid over it? Did a paper fall off the desk and then fly under it? Did you put it away where it belonged and forget you did that?

As you search, look slowly, calmly, thoroughly. Concentrate on what you need. Consider alternative visual images (maybe it was short and thick instead of long and thin). Think positive thoughts: "I know I can find it. I'll just stay cool-headed and it'll show up right away."

Negative thoughts impede your chances of success. Level-headedness, focusing, and positive thoughts will greatly improve your chances of locating what you need.

SUMMARY

- *Visualize how beautiful things will look and how good you'll feel when you get everything organized.*
- *Develop an organizing system that fits your style.*
- *Start somewhere! Rough sorting is an easy way to begin.*
- *Designate a specific time for sorting, avoid distractions, and stick to it.*
- *Multi-compartment boxes help make sorting fast and easy. Let categories evolve as you sort.*
- *Use headings that make sense to you.*
- *Watch out for paper clips!*
- *Follow each action with a reaction.*
- *Open your mail near a wastebasket and pitch envelopes now!*
- *Make important notations on your calendar as you open your mail.*
- *In looking for lost items, take a moment to calm down and focus on the item, not on self-demeaning statements.*

12

PLOWING A PATH
THROUGH PERSONAL PAPERS

The preceding chapter focused on the general aspects of paper handling; this one will deal with specific methods for handling papers at home.

The Management Center
Because of the growing abundance of necessary paperwork involved in running every home, we believe that home business matters should be run like a regular business. With insurance papers, bills to pay, tax returns, banking, investment reports, important papers on real estate, cars, and other properties (to say nothing of everyday mail, children's papers, magazines, catalogs, brochures, and so on), it is becoming almost imperative that a central "management center" be established in the home.

Without a central location to maintain necessary papers, this miscellanea can become *mess*ellanea instead. That is, papers tend to become scattered about the house. Then, when a telephone call requires reference to bills, schedules, or insurance coverage, for instance, you may end up scooting from one room to another before you locate the item in question.

The best place for this management center is often the kitchen, unless an immediately adjoining room, such as a library, office, or den with desk space, is available. Although we admit we'd prefer to locate this center elsewhere, in practice the kitchen is still the center of most homes; it's where most telephone calls are taken, and consequently it's where information should be available at one's fingertips.

Create a "management center" by your telephone where you keep papers, bills, and supplies you often use.

If you have a home-based business, you'll need to establish an actual office in a converted bedroom, basement room, or other separate space. For general home-related matters, however, there are two problems with trying to have the home management center elsewhere: First, when mail or other papers come into the home, they usually get put down in the kitchen or somewhere else close by. Then, regardless of one's good intentions to take those papers to the remote desk location, the papers instead tend to end up scattered between the place where they first entered the house and their ultimate destination.

Second, when a phone call comes that requires reference to those papers, the call is still taken in the kitchen, but the papers are then in a remote part of the house. This simply doesn't work.

Be sure the location of your management center is in an area where you like to work. If you try to squeeze your paper-working area into a space facing a dark corner, you may find that spot claustrophobic and avoid working there without realizing why.

Even the color of the room can affect you. If you have a room beautifully decorated in celery green, but you're not a "celery green person," you may want to escape from that room the first chance you get—again without understanding why. You'll only vaguely know that you have a feeling of wanting to get out of there. If you already dislike doing paperwork and then try to work on it in a place that's unpleasant for you, you'll never get it done!

Necessities

There are only a few basic necessities for a good management center: a properly lighted desk area, adequate supplies, a telephone, and a filing system for holding your papers in an orderly manner.

The Desk. Your desk doesn't have to be a formal, executive-style desk. The kitchen table will do fine, *if* it offers quick access to the other items listed above. So long as the desk provides a smooth writing surface with space to spread out your working papers and you can reach whatever else you need without getting up, that's all that's necessary.

For a formal desk at home or in your office, we suggest you arrange it so that papers can "flow through." In other words, if you are right-handed, arrange your "in" box or other receiving spot of your desk to your left. Work on your papers in the center of your desk, of course, and keep your "out" box, files, and wastebasket to your right, so that papers just naturally flow in from the left and out to the right. (Reverse this order if you are left-handed.)

An inexpensive but effective desk can easily be fashioned by laying a flat door over a pair of two-drawer filing cabinets, leaving knee space in between.

Supplies. If you want to handle your paperwork in the shortest possible time, you'll need adequate supplies. If you constantly have to make trips (either to the next room or to the store) to get what you need to accomplish a task, make a concerted effort to keep all the supplies you need right where you work.

Lack of proper supplies can delay your paperwork without your even realizing it. Perhaps you need to mail a large set of papers to a friend, but keep putting it off. You may not even realize that (1) You don't have envelopes big enough to hold the papers; (2) you don't have a postage scale, so you don't know how much postage is required; and (3) you don't have larger denominations of stamps on hand.

Drop by your local office-supply store and browse for supplies that will work for you, so that you'll have on hand what you need when you need it. To use our examples from the previous chapter, Linda would keep all her equipment neatly tucked away in her desk drawers, with extras in a nearby supply cabinet, while Ryan would want them out in plain sight on top of his desk.

If you don't have drawer or cabinet space for your supplies, the next best alternative is to keep them in a box in a cupboard or closet and only bring them out when you sit down to do your paperwork, then return them to the storage place when you're done. Many good organizing tools are available to help you set up your own system, but once again we emphasize: Buy only organizers that fit your specific needs, and beware of adding more items that will only add to your clutter.

The Telephone. The telephone is needed to receive calls in a place where you can refer to your current action papers, and it's very handy to have a phone available to make calls when you have questions about papers you're handling.

The "Filing" System. The main consideration for storing papers is easy retrievability. You want to store your papers so they are easy to put away at first and easy to get out when you need them again; therefore, setting up your personal filing or cubbyhole system requires a little thought. Consider first what type of system you want to use, and, second, where it will be located. We put the word "filing" in quotes because if you're an Arbie you may not want to use a standard filing system. Instead, a cubbyhole arrangement similar to the sorter discussed in the previous chapter may be right for you. This can be placed inside a kitchen cupboard or on top of a counter or other surface area that's handy.

If you aren't adverse to filing, we suggest establishing actual filing drawers in your kitchen. This suggestion often evokes immediate objections: "I don't want a filing cabinet or an ugly sorter in my kitchen. That would look awful!" Our only reply is "Well, yes, maybe you're right. But if you have stacks of papers on your kitchen counters, how do they look?" Sometimes it becomes a matter not of what looks perfect, but rather of what looks least bad.

Be creative in eyeing possible filing places in your kitchen. Ideally, you could have file drawers built right into your kitchen cabinets. If that's impractical or unaffordable for you, however, the filing cabinet may be your next best alternative. One of our consulting clients insisted she didn't have space for a filing cabinet, yet she had a TV sitting on a little table in the corner of her eating area. By replacing the table with an attractive filing cabinet, her lack of filing space was solved almost like magic.

Also remember that there are ways of camouflaging filing cabinets. For example, you can turn an unsightly two-drawer filing cabinet into an attractive "table" by placing a circular piece of plywood atop the cabinet and covering it with a lovely floor-length tablecloth—which can actually add beauty to your home or office. The cloth can then just be folded up and back for access to the filing folders.

Filing cabinets now come in every possible color and size. You can get them in white, almond, wood-grain, pastels, or vivid decorator colors. They are manufactured in every material from cardboard to fine wood. As a rule, you get what you pay for in filing cabinets. We recommend getting something that is sturdy enough to last many years, and lockable if that is important to you.

Be aware that filing cabinets come in varying depths, and most drawers have about six inches of "dead" space in the back end. The heights of filing cabinets also vary, so if you are looking for a two-drawer cabinet to fit under a table or the knee hole of a desk, shop around until you find one to fit the space available.

Many people file their papers in colorful "milk crates." Some of these crates are made specifically to hold hanging folders, are about the most economical way of filing papers, are easily transportable, and are very practical for people like college students. If you use those crates, you may want to keep handy something attractive (such as an afghan) to cover them when needed, since open filing tends to have a cluttered appearance. A coverup also protects the files from toddlers, pets, and dust.

Periodicals

Do you have stacks of unread periodicals in your home or office? If you're "normal," you probably do, because this seems to be one of the universal problems the authors see. It seems to be a sign of the times that everyone wants to be well informed, so they subscribe to many periodicals, yet, regardless of all good intentions, they don't have time to read them.

Since all good "savers" are conservative people who want to make sure they get good use out of the things they buy, they save those newsletters and magazines until they get around to reading them—which in some cases is not only later but never! Here are some insights regarding the saving of these unread publications.

First of all, just because you bought them doesn't mean you are duty-bound to read them. You probably don't read the *Washington Post* and *The New York Times* and the *Chicago Tribune* and the *Los Angeles Times*. There are fifty thousand books published every year. (And we're glad you found this one!) You get the picture—you can't read everything, so relax! If you don't read it, it's okay. Life will go on and you'll still be well informed.

We had one friend in Chicago who became aware she was spending too many hours reading the *Chicago Tribune* and wasn't getting enough done. She purposely dropped her subscription to the paper because it was too good—and put her time to better use by going back to school. She then made it a point to watch the TV news and she subscribed to a weekly news magazine, so that she could be informed without spending undue time reading.

If you subscribe to a magazine for the purpose of gathering specific information you want to keep, rather than keeping the whole journal, try tearing out all the advertising. Since seventy percent of the average magazine is made up of ads, doing this can reduce its size to about thirty percent of its original volume. Then store the magazine upright on a shelf, in a vertical magazine holder, for easy future reference. We recommend retaining only very specific magazines, however. The lion's share of magazines need to go. If you need to refer back to something you threw out, you can always go to the library to retrieve it. (In fact, you might find it faster there!)

Many people save magazines because they think that someone else could "make good use of them." This is fine, but remember that until you deliver them to someone else, no one else can be using them!

We recommend taking stock of the unread periodicals you have on hand right now. Be honest with yourself—there is a reason you haven't read them. Three reasons would probably rank high:

1. You "haven't had time" to look at them yet. You probably just aren't interested enough, yet you feel guilty for not reading them. So why are you paying good money to buy guilt for yourself? Write to the magazine company and ask for a refund for the rest of your unused subscription term, saying you aren't reading the magazine, so you'd like your money back. This may take a couple of months, but it will solve your problem. On others, just don't renew your subscription. With less incoming mail, you'll have fewer demands on your time.

2. There's a particular article you want to read and/or save. Make up a reading basket or folder and keep it by your bedside or easy chair. As you look through magazines and notice articles you want to read or keep, tear them out right then and place them in your reading holder. (If another family member hasn't read that magazine yet, they'll know to look in your reading file if something is missing.) One woman we know doesn't subscribe to even one women's magazine. However, when she occasionally sees a specific one on a store shelf that interests her, she'll readily pay newsstand price for it. Even though she pays more once in a while, she saves money in the long run and doesn't have a pileup of unread magazines at home.

For the newspapers, magazines, and newsletters you do subscribe to, *provide a limited amount of space to keep them, and no more.* Or perhaps you can keep the last two issues of each subscription. When the next issue comes in, the oldest one goes out—read or unread. (Don't worry—with today's information explosion, you'll still have plenty to read.)

Article Clippings

The percentage of organizing seminar participants who suffer from this particular malady is amazingly high. Typically, people tear out an article they want to keep and lay it in a stack of "stuff"—where it remains indefinitely. If you're interested in keeping article clippings—and there's nothing wrong with that, *if you really do go back and refer to them from time to time*—then set up a method for storing and retrieving them: files for Elbies, cubbyholes for Arbies. When a category accumulates enough papers to merit a cubbyhole, label it with a subject category: "Health and Fitness"; "Gardening"; "Children"; "Traveling"; and perhaps one for "Miscellaneous Articles." (Be very careful of what you put there, so it doesn't become overgrown.)

Before you actually file another article, however, give some careful thought to whether you actually utilize your saved articles or if you save them just because "you might need them sometime." Often, when you go back over the articles you clipped out earlier, you'll wonder why you even saved them in the first place. The fact is, you were in another frame of mind when you first cut it out than you were when you returned to it.

Also, in our fast-paced society, information becomes obsolete almost as soon as it's disseminated. What seemed true yesterday may not be true today. Don't *hoard* information today that you'll be *bored* with tomorrow!

Catalogs/Brochures/Maps

Information descends upon us in an unending variety of sizes and shapes. Maps, brochures, catalogs, and other materials accumulate into bulky, sliding messes that make retention difficult. We suggest several possibilities:

- The cubbyhole grouping can hold a great deal of odd-sized clutter in easily accessible order.
- Hanging folders are now made in three-sided, accordion-style "box bottom folders" to hold odd-shaped literature.
- Various kinds of vertical magazine holders are handy for holding maps, travel brochures, catalogs, and so forth. We recommend buying inexpensive corrugated holders and putting these kinds of reference items on a closed-in shelf or in a rough storage area. They look neat that way, yet you can find what you need almost immediately.

Photos

Do you have photos scattered about in various spots in your home—some in albums, some in boxes, others in your desk drawer, and still more in miscellaneous catchalls? If so, again, you are pretty typical. Ideally, of course, every photo you have ever taken is neatly labeled and inserted in order in an acetate, polyester, or polypropylene album. (Never put your photographs in pages of albums made of polyvinyl chloride, or PVC. This material will leach the color from your pictures and in time they will fade into extinction. Check the label of any new albums you purchase and check your old ones to observe the condition of your older photos. If they are fading, pull them out quickly and replace them in "safe" materials!)

If your pictures aren't organized, we'd like to suggest an interim step between complete disorganization and the final album stage—one that will keep them safe and in order until you have time to sit down and "do it right."

Secure some kind of box—a shoe box, a five-by-eight-inch card-file box from the office-supply store, or any other similar-sized container. Make or buy dividers to fit, and mark them according to year. As you come across pictures scattered around your home or office, take the time right then to label them on the back. (Or put them by your favorite chair to label while you're watching TV tonight.) You may not remember everyone's name, but your memory isn't going to get better tomorrow, so do what you can right now.

If you still have the envelopes in which the photos came back from the processor, label the outsides of the envelopes with the dates and general places the pictures were taken, and place the envelopes holding both your pictures and negatives behind the appropriate year-dated dividers. This is less than ideal, but it's a practical and nonthreatening intermediate way to keep your photos safe and orderly until you have time to give them better attention. In the meantime they won't get damaged, curled, or faded.

Children's Papers and the Refrigerator

If you have preschool or grade-school children, you know about the overabundance of childhood papers that rapidly accumulates. If your children's papers tend to clutter up many spots in the house, provide a specific "in" box to receive the daily papers that deserve your attention. Spend a little time every day or two going over those papers with your child, and teach him or her not to be a saver. It's appropriate to keep a few samples of the child's work, but it's unnecessary to save every paper!

If you enjoy making scrapbooks with your children, that's wonderful. Too often, however, the good intentions of making scrapbooks end up with piles of disorganized "stuff." We suggest making a file or cubbyhole for each child. Collect some papers throughout the school year and, at the end of the year, sort out those papers with your child and select which few items can be kept permanently, throwing out the rest. Then move those papers from your kitchen management center to a storage area in the child's room, basement, attic, or other appropriate place. Retain the same folder or cubbyhole for next year.

Everyone knows that the refrigerator has become the Great American Children's Art Gallery. A word about the refrigerator, though: We think it's lovely that parents are willing to exhibit and admire their children's works of art. (We have even known college students who put their own A-plus papers on the fronts of their dorm refrigerators!) Be aware, however, that although your children's papers may look beautiful to you, an accumulation of them may look messy to others.

The problem with putting children's art up on the refrigerator is getting it down again! Too often the parents (or grandparents) don't want to hurt the child's feelings, so they leave the work up indefinitely. Here are some suggestions to alleviate the problem:

- Rather than the refrigerator, put up a bulletin board where the family can see it and close friends can be taken to see it.
- Agree with your children upon a length of time for art to be displayed. After a few days it can be removed to a file, or displayed in the child's room.
- Designate one spot on the refrigerator (or in a special frame along a hallway, for instance) for each child, where *only his or her latest project* is always on display.

Part of a child's education is to learn that he or she *can't keep everything forever,* that saving a reasonable number of prized possessions is healthy, but keeping everything is not.

Recipes
Recipes torn from newspapers and magazines seem to be another universal type of clutter problem. Here's a typical scenario:

In a magazine you see a picture of a dish that looks mouth-wateringly good. You decide you'd like to try it, so you tear the recipe out. The next time you're expecting guests for dinner, you confidently whip out that recipe, look it over, and then realize you've never tried it before. Suddenly your confidence diminishes as you wonder, "What if it isn't as good as it looks?" Since it's not a good idea to use dinner guests as guinea pigs, you decide that perhaps you'd best try it out first on your family, and stick with your tried-and-true favorites. Then, when it's time to cook the family dinner (a disappearing phenomenon in our society), you excuse yourself because you're too tired or you don't want to go to that much trouble and the recipe remains untested and unused.

We do have one really great suggestion for all the recipes you have torn out and never used: Put them all together in an attractive box. Tie them securely with a pretty ribbon, make a nice bow on the top, and label them carefully. Then use them as a boat anchor. . . .

Seriously, if you're determined to "get good use" out of the recipes you've saved, select one to three of those recipes and test them out *this week*. Those that you don't test (despite your good intentions) get thrown out, along with those, of course, that don't turn out well. Gradually go through your recipes this way, making notations on them about special information that would be helpful the next time you use them, and then retain them in an orderly manner. There are innumerable methods you can use to save recipes:

- Copy them onto a three-by-five or five-by-eight card and keep them in a recipe box with appropriate dividers.
- Affix them onto plain paper sheets in a loose-leaf binder, with dividers for "Appetizers," "Beverages," "Bread," and so forth.
- Put them into a photo album—again divided appropriately.
- Maintain a pocket folder with each page pocket designated for the different categories.

The Shopping List

Don't wait until it's time to go shopping before starting to make a shopping list. Keep a running list as you use up items or notice that things in your pantry are running low. Train your family to do the same. Teach children too young to write to simply place the empty container (of peanut butter, for instance) in a certain spot in your kitchen so you'll notice and add it to the list yourself.

We also recommend making a permanent shopping list. Write, in columns, all the items you might normally buy, leaving some blanks, and laminate the paper or insert it into a clear plastic holder. Use a china marker—also known as a grease pencil—to mark items you need during the week as you run out of them. (These supplies are available at office supply stores.) Your shopping will go faster if you arrange your list in the same order in which the items are found in your supermarket. Then sit down the night before you go shopping, plan your weekly menu, add those remaining items to your list, and you'll be well prepared to head off to the store the next day.

When you return, simply wipe the "slate" clean with a dry tissue or paper towel, and your list will be ready for the next week's list.

Incidentally, we recommend that you go to the grocery store *no more than once each week.* Shopping more often can be a waste of time and money, since you'll doubtless spend more on inviting foods you hadn't intended to buy.

Coupons

Ah, yes—then there are discount coupons. Nature's scourge to some shoppers! We realize, of course, that many, many people save lots of money with coupons, so we don't want to put down or offend anyone who takes advantage of them. For those who don't, however, coupons really can be a guilt-producing scourge. The very nature of the lowly coupon is to make the consumer feel guilty if he or she isn't "smart enough" to take advantage of them. Here are some typical scenarios:

- You spend lots of time organizing your coupons at home, only to find at the store counter that you left them at home or in your car.
- You studiously search out and collect each product, only to find—to the clerk's suspicious eye and to your embarrassment—that the obscure dates on your coupons have expired!
- The coupons slide out of your hand all over the grocery store floor—and then you find that your store doesn't have several of the items you wanted to collect on.
- You find that you can buy the house brand more cheaply than the expensive brand with the coupon—after all, the cost of advertising is why it's so expensive in the first place!
- You end up buying extra items you don't really need, just to take advantage of the coupon.

Though many people do indeed save a good deal of money on coupons, if they don't work for you, don't worry about them. Forget them! In fact, *we hereby give you permission never to feel guilty about throwing coupons away again.* (There. Did that help?) The fact is that in many cases your time is more valuable than the few cents you save on a coupon. We suggest some alternatives:

- Don't use any coupons. (God will not strike you dead for this, we promise.)
- Use only those coupons for brands you would buy anyway.
- Keep only coupons of relatively high value. (Set your own lower limit.)

Set aside specific times to deal with coupons on a regular basis, and throw out any you don't have time for.

SUMMARY

- *Set up a management center with all you'll need for everyday affairs.*
- *You can't read everything, so set a limited amount of space or a limited amount of time for keeping periodicals.*
- *Be selective about how many clippings you keep and where you keep them.*
- *Find holders that would be suitable for storing oddly shaped materials.*
- *Keep photos in a designated covered box until you can get them into an album.*
- *Limit the number and length of time children's papers will be kept on the refrigerator and in storage.*
- *Limit the number and length of time unused recipes will be kept.*
- *Limit the number and length of time you'll keep coupons.*

13

THE INNER STRUGGLE

In previous chapters we have discussed different personality types and organizing styles. In this chapter and the one following we will address the inner obstacles one must overcome. We'll also discuss some of the difficulties or challenges that face opposite types of people when they happen to connect with each other—whether they are married, work together, or for any other reason must deal with each other's organizing styles. We'll offer guidelines for considering how to change, as well as for giving and receiving criticism between individuals with differing organizing styles.

The Uphill Battle

In Greek mythology, Sisyphus was condemned to push a huge stone to the top of a hill. With great physical exertion he pushed and pushed all day long until he got the stone all the way to the top. But no sooner had he reached the top than the stone rolled all the way back down to the bottom. Sisyphus then had to begin his effort all over again.

This story may sound familiar because the struggle to stay organized is always an uphill battle. Many times throughout your lifetime you may "push the stone all the way up to the top of the hill," look around, and say, "This is great! I made it. Everything I possess is in perfect order!"

But what happens? You "release the stone," and the next thing you know, you look around and things are once again in disarray. It can be extremely discouraging to realize how long it takes to straighten up clutter, and what a short time it takes for the clutter to collect again.

All or Nothing

Why is this? Partly because when Arbies do decide to change their own behavior, they tend to take an all-or-nothing approach. If you're an Arbie you won't say, for example, "I'm going to file this one stack of papers." Instead you'll say, "I'm going to sort out this whole five-year accumulation of papers and magazines and have everything looking perfect." At that point you may well work night and day until it's all done, and become completely exhausted in the process. Then you're likely to switch to the opposite mode, doing no cleaning or straightening, and before long the same kind of clutter will have accumulated again.

The tendency to take the all-or-nothing approach is reminiscent of Sisyphus. You may work and work with intense effort to get the clutter under control and then say with a sigh, "I don't have to worry about that anymore." And that's your downfall. As soon as you say that, you begin the "down side" of your Sisyphus Syndrome, and little by little the stone rolls down until you are at the bottom again and you find things have gained on you because you haven't been paying attention on a consistent basis.

How Self-Concept Is Affected by Being an Arbie

It's amazing that sometimes people can go on seemingly pushing stones up hills day after day, only to release them and then push them back up again. Why should a person continue to live in such a fashion? The answer lies in the basic human tendency to cling to the familiar.

This concept was dramatically illustrated at the end of World War II, when the gates of concentration camps were thrown open and prisoners who had endured the most horrible conditions were liberated. They rushed out into their newfound freedom, but some of them turned around and walked back inside!

Why would they do that? Since it's difficult to change our

patterns of behavior, we tend to stay in the same old routines of doing things in certain ways because they are familiar.

"Yeah, but . . ."

When we counsel Arbies about the benefits of developing left-brain organizing skills, they often voice concerns such as, "Yeah, but I don't went to lose the child in me," or "Yeah, but I don't want to be so structured that I lose all my spontaneity."

Of course, in the reverse situation an Elbie will argue, "Yeah, but I just can't live without structure in my life," or "Yeah, but I just can't rest until everything is put away properly."

Of all the normal verbal reactions any counselor hears, "Yeah, but" is probably the most common. These "Yeah, buts" are important. They reflect resistances—the internal conflicts a person has within himself or herself.

> Aaron was very worried that keeping his desk in order would turn him into the kind of person he had always scorned—uptight, rigid, never spontaneous. Aaron was very creative and somewhat flamboyant, full of energy and creativity. He had a great sense of humor, and he definitely didn't want to become "Mr. Pinstriped Suit."
>
> Aaron was also concerned about the time it would take to put his desk in order and keep it that way, so we examined this. When asked how much time he spent searching for things, the smile of recognition was immediate and he realized that by taking ten minutes faithfully every single day to clear off his desk, he would be saving himself endless hours that he had previously spent looking for this or that—an odd scrap of paper, his scissors, or a telephone number, for instance.
>
> It would have been fun to videotape the expression on his face when he realized he wouldn't be losing his true self by keeping things in order—that he could still be his spontaneous, wonderful, right-brain self.
>
> When he realized he would just be making his own life a little easier and less chaotic, a flood of relief poured

over him. He understood for the first time that he could have the best of both worlds. By continuing to be his creative, relaxed self and, in addition, adding on other skills, he could make his life easier and more effective without taking anything away.

Developing Your Self-Management Skills

When you're young, you have a parent or guardian to set limits for you, to nurture you, to make sure you do all the things that are necessary to be healthy physically, mentally, and emotionally. Part of the process of maturing is learning how to develop your own self-management skills and become a parent to yourself. You need to learn how to do for yourself all the things that a parent did for you as a child.

Before this process is complete, however, there are often struggles between parent and child. For example, when a little boy is told by his mother to do something—say, to clean up toys—perhaps he just doesn't feel like doing it. So his mother says, "I want you to do that," and the child says, "I don't want to," and his mother says, "But you have to," and the child says, "I won't," and his parent says, "I'm going to make you," and the child says, "Oh yeah? Try it!" Very quickly, both parties are digging in their heels in a classic power struggle.

As people mature physically, they sometimes remain involved in a power struggle, even though the parent may live far away and may not even know what the individual is doing. These grown men and women are still doing or not doing things simply out of compliance with, or defiance of, their parents' wishes. Unfortunately, many people develop this critical, authoritative aspect of the parent figure, but not the nurturing side. Many people literally need to learn how to nurture themselves.

Shoulds and Oughts

By the time you're an adult, you have learned, we hope, to govern your own behavior. Most people are pretty good at criticizing or scolding themselves when they "misbehave." They are also pretty good at telling themselves (as their parents used to) what they "should," "ought to," or "have to" do.

As soon as you get into *shoulds, ought-to's,* or *have-to's,* the other part of you is going to rebel. When you start to say to yourself, "I really *should* clear off the top of my desk," "I really *must* clean out my basement," and so forth, the other half of you will reply, "Yeah, I really *ought to* do that—but I don't want to."

As long as there is a part of you saying "you have to," "you must," or "you should," that's the parent part of you talking— and as surely as night follows day, the little kid within you is going to come back with a wink and say, "I'll betcha I can get out of it," or "I'll betcha I don't have to." And so the inner dialogue goes back and forth.

Intrapersonal Conflict

Many people's perception is that these *shoulds* and *ought-to's* are *inter*personal conflicts—battles between oneself and another person—when in reality the battle is *intra*personal— within conflicting parts of the self. The conflict is not between me, who wants one thing, and somebody else—mother, father, supervisor, kids—who wants something else, but rather within the self. When you can acknowledge that your conflict is from within, you can get a handle on your own behavior, because that acknowledgment eliminates all the useless power struggles.

Rebelling Against Pressure

Rather than rebelling directly against doing something like cleaning up, some people rebel passively by resisting lists, clocks, calendars, and deadlines. They may not want to be tied to anything that is conceivably causing pressure on them to do their tasks, and will purposely defy such regimentation of their life. Instead, they want to be spontaneous.

In reality, getting things done before the deadline actually gives you more control. When you decide to get things done before pressure is put on you by others, you feel more in charge of your own life. It's only when you refuse to manage your own work that control from others becomes a factor at all.

It's unfortunate when a person believes he is being "cute" by "getting away with" not doing his work, perhaps as a way of rebelling against authority, even long after the authority figure is no longer involved in his life. Instead, we invite you to reassess and take a more mature, responsible position in life. After all, it is only yourself that you are sabotaging.

Guilt

If you say, "I really *should* clear off my desk," you aren't recognizing you've actually made a decision *not* to do this work. You're saying, "I really *should*, but I'm not gonna—but I *am* going to feel guilty about it. *And because I feel guilty about it, I must be a conscientious person.*" In a way, you're fooling yourself.

Someone has said, "Guilt is giving ourselves permission to keep on doing what we are doing." Think about that: When you feel guilty for not clearing off your desk, you're giving yourself permission to keep on not clearing it off.

When you feel guilty about something, stop and deal with the guilt. Stop everything and decide either to do it and forget it, or *not* to do it and forget it, and not feel guilty about it. *But make your choice a conscious choice.* Don't try to fool yourself. If you say right out, "I'm not going to clean that garage," or "I'm not going to clear the clutter," then you've made a decision. You've stated it, and that's that—it's settled—and you have come to terms with the fact this is something you have chosen not to do.

Choice

Whenever you say, "I have to do that," ask yourself, "*Why* do I have to do that? What makes me think I have to do it?"

You'll probably answer, "I have to because I want to get certain results." That changes the statement. The statement is now, "If I want *A*, then I have to do *B*"—and that statement alone can make a tremendous difference in your life. Then you need to decide whether or not you really want to do it.

In dealing with inner resistance, it's extremely important to make that statement: "If I want to, then I have to—but do I really want to?" It's not unusual for a person to be pulled in two directions at once. One part of you wants to do one thing—make a social phone call, for instance—while another voice within says you "should" be working.

Realistic Expectations

When someone comes to us and says, "I'm just totally over-whelmed. I have stuff stacked from the floor to the ceiling and I just couldn't possibly get all that stuff cleaned up," we ask the individual, "How many years has it taken you to accumulate all this mess?" They might say five, ten, or twenty years, and we say, "How long do you think it will take to organize it?" If they say one or two weeks, we will say that's unrealistic. If they say, "I couldn't be ready to move in five years," that's unrealistic, too.

The reality is that to organize a lifetime of clutter that has accumulated over a period of ten, twenty, or more years, realistically it will take many, many hours of work—but not years, no matter what shape it's gotten into.

Accepting Your Own Limitations

It may be extremely difficult to accept your limitations and keep from kidding yourself into thinking, "I can do every-thing." Some people tend to take on more than they can handle and then end up saying, "I'm inadequate because I can't do all this."

If you are one of these people, consider this: You *are* inadequate to the task! You are pretending to be able to do things far beyond human capabilities! If you were to sit down with another person and look honestly at what you are expecting of yourself, with your resources and skills, it would be immediately obvious your expectations were unreasonable.

Assessing Realistic Versus Unrealistic Expectations

Unrealistic expectations of yourself can also immobilize you with anxiety. Many Arbies continue thinking they "should" be able to do something when they aren't able to, and therefore get so overwhelmed by feelings of inadequacy, discourage-ment, and resentment that they end up wasting time whirling around in these negative feelings instead of digging in and doing the task at hand. This is a miserable way to live, and it's very stress-producing, so learning to set realistic goals is extremely important.

When you talk about your frustration in not being organized, you must first consider your overall life circumstances in order to sort out what you can realistically hope to achieve. What you can expect of yourself now may be very different from what you may have been able to do ten years ago, or what you might expect of yourself five years from now. Perhaps your health has changed in recent years or you'll be able to acquire new education in the future that will make your life easier. Therefore, you need to ask yourself some questions:

1. To what degree are you right-brain dominant? You would need to look at your own limitations in these terms, because it isn't realistic to expect an extreme Arbie to switch over suddenly and become an excessively well-organized person.

2. What are your resources? What you can realistically hope to achieve when you live in a spacious home with lots of storage space, a housekeeper, no children, and a cooperative mate would be very different from what you might expect of yourself if you were living in a small home with little storage space, several children, and no help from a housekeeper or a partner.

3. If someone else were in this same situation, what would you expect of them? See if perhaps you're expecting a lot more of yourself than you would of someone else in similar circumstances, given the same amount of resources as are available to you.

4. What would be totally unrealistic to expect of yourself? Try exaggerating to the extreme. Begin exaggerating all the ridiculous things you might expect yourself to accomplish in the next three hours, for instance. After recognizing how impossible your exaggerations would be to accomplish, you will be more attuned to what is realistic *in terms of this particular task,* given the amount of resources you have.

Take some time to get in touch with what is sensible to expect of yourself in organizational tasks, specifically use of time, management of clutter, and so on. Focusing on realistic expectations helps to focus your energy.

Comparison with Others

It's important to learn never to compare yourself with other people; it's never helpful or healthy. There will always be someone who is superior to you in whatever aspect of yourself you will be comparing. And there will be others who are inferior to you. If you want to feel superior or inferior, then go ahead and compare, but what good does it do? The truth is that being organized and staying organized is far more difficult for some individuals than for others. There are people who have a natural knack for organizing, and since it's not difficult for them, they may just naturally expect that it should be easy for others as well.

Discouragement

Another obstacle that people often struggle with is discouragement. If you look around and discover that once again you are in the midst of clutter you've created, you may be inclined to berate yourself, saying things like, "It's no use. I'm just a failure. No matter how much I struggle, I'm always going to backslide. I'm hopeless," and on and on.

These messages do two things: First, they sap you of energy, since "down" messages produce "down" feelings. Second, the time you spend berating yourself (which can last anywhere from a few moments to a chronic, ongoing process) is time spent avoiding the job that needs to be done.

When you find yourself spending time drowning in feelings of self-loathing or self-pity, don't berate yourself for having these feelings *in addition* to berating yourself for not getting the job done! Develop the habit at moments like this of saying one word: "Oops!" This means that you allow yourself one second to acknowledge that you have slipped off track. Then stubbornly refuse to waste any additional time wallowing. Instead, pitch in.

When you can focus on what needs to be done, it turns your attention outward, allowing you to concentrate on your work or play. When you are focused on your activities rather than on yourself, you are naturally going to be more productive. Even measuring your progress needs to be limited, because progress may be uneven. Perhaps one day you'll make a lot of progress, and the next day you may fall back a little and the day after that you may make more progress again. One of the most difficult things is for people to learn to be kind to themselves.

Fears

Freud remarked that to complete all tasks is to die. The projects that we are involved in give meaning to our lives. One of the reasons people delay finishing projects is that they dread the lack of meaning that follows when they have finished one thing and have not yet launched another. Many of us feel we need our work around us in order to feel important. If we have nothing to do, then we tend to fear that we aren't important. For example, there are mothers who invest their whole self-esteem in being needed by their children. When their children grow up and leave the home, certain women have a difficult time "finding themselves" because they no longer feel "needed" or "important." In other cases, people tend to leave work to be done in obvious places in order to look important. Their fear is not that they don't have anything important to do, but that others will think they don't. Take the actual case of our friend Tom, for instance:

> Tom was a real estate broker who had a huge executive desk completely covered with intermingled piles of papers from one to six inches high, topped with years of dust. He used to lean back in his high-backed executive chair, take a puff on his big cigar, and brag to his secretary, "You see, all these papers on my desk make me look important when these big New York brokers come in to see me. It makes me look like I've got lots of big deals going." ("Important" would not have been his secretary's choice of words to describe how it made Tom look.)

Anxiety

One of the most common emotions that affect organizational abilities is anxiety. Being in a cluttered environment may be anxiety-producing for some people. Each time they see the clutter, their anxiety level goes up. Thus they believe that the anxiety is the result of the clutter, and indeed it may be. But the clutter may also be the *result* of the anxiety in some cases.

When an individual is suffering from anxiety, he or she may find it difficult to focus effectively on tasks. You yourself may be able to recall an episode of anxiety—slight or severe, brief or prolonged. It would not be unusual for you to have produced clutter at such a time by absentmindedly picking things up and setting them down again with no thought whatever to where you have put them. (Some people, in moments of anxiety, go to the opposite extreme of becoming "super neat," but this is not our concern here.) Your environment, then, may be a reflection of your internal anxieties.

Teenagers can serve as a prime example of this problem. When teenagers encounter changes in their lives—as they suddenly grow taller and mature physically and their hormones go wild—they often experience enormous anxieties. At the same time, they may let a formerly neat bedroom become a litter of clothes, books, CDs, and every kind of assorted paraphernalia. One teen told his mother, "My room looks just like my mind feels."

"Good" teenagers who are not rebelling in the street will often rebel about cleaning up their rooms as an expression of normal rebellious feelings that they experience during this period. Although a child should never be allowed to "trash" a home, this is not the time to lose good communication with your teen over the neatness of his or her own room.

Depression

Another emotional state that affects organizational skills is depression. Depression may be so extreme that it can cause an almost vegetative state, or so mild as to be hardly noticeable. It can sometimes be the result of suppressed anger. One reaction to depression is inertia or immobilization—the extent of which will depend on the depth of the depression. When you're emotionally upset, you're probably focusing on what's upsetting you rather than concentrating on what needs to be done. You may feel overwhelmed, helpless. Your thinking may become unclear, scattered, and fragmented. This is when you're likely to do your poorest or least important work. You might even become "paralyzed" in your ability to accomplish anything. Even if you are active, you might not actually be getting anything accomplished. This situation might be compared to a centipede lying on its back, flailing all its legs but going nowhere.

It's important to recognize that even mild states of depression or other emotional turmoil can affect you. Even if you only get a little low every now and then, don't expect so much of yourself that day. Find easy work that you can do almost automatically—tasks that don't require a great deal of concentration or decision making. *Forgive yourself* on those days for not accomplishing as much as you might. These little reprieves will act as a refresher so that you can come back stronger the next day.

Don't relive, again and again, negative aspects of your life. Brooding about how trapped you feel, how much of a victim you are, or other imagined difficulties only perpetuates bad situations. Concentrate on positives and remove negative thinking as much as possible.

Some depression is, of course, natural. The death of a loved one, divorce, or other major negative changes will cause natural periods of grieving that should be accepted. When these periods extend beyond normal limits, however, something more must be done.

Physical activity *will* decrease depression. The problem is that many people who are already in this state feel incapable of getting themselves moving. If this is the case, it's necessary to pinpoint the area of stress. One older woman came to an organizing class and complained that she had raised five children, kept a large house without help, worked with her husband in his business, and never had organizing problems. Now her husband was dead and her children were grown and had moved away. She had moved into a small condo and, she lamented, she couldn't even keep that clean. She was apparently suffering from depression and a feeling of being unimportant or unneeded. Just realizing how her depression had affected her reassured her that she wasn't becoming senile. She was then able to concentrate on recovering from her depressed state, and her condo clutter improved in the process.

Another young woman had three preschoolers, and everything about her demeanor literally shouted depression: slumped body, straggly hair, no makeup, dowdy clothes, even slurred speech—and she complained that her house was a "wreck." During an organizing class she realized that depression was contributing to her disorganization. After dealing with her depression, she enrolled in a computer-programming class, and a year later she was seen dressed in high style, her speech and demeanor lively and vibrant—and she proudly proclaimed that her house was one hundred percent better organized.

Keep in mind that *when you do something for yourself, you do something for your mental health.*

If you experience ongoing depression, however, or if it intensifies despite your self-help efforts, remember that there are qualified mental-health professionals in your area who are trained in helping people recover from depression.

Being an Imperfectionist

Many times, people are reluctant to dig in and actually begin a task because they have the attitude that "either I'm going to do it perfectly or I'm going to wait until I have the time and energy and skill and everything else to do it perfectly."

G. K. Chesterton, the English author, said, "If it's worth doing at all, it's worth doing poorly," which of course is the paradox: if we only did the things that we could do perfectly, we wouldn't do much. So part of the resistance within us is involved in accepting our limitations—that at this particular moment, given the amount of time, energy, space, and money available to me, this is the best that I can do. This means making a conscious choice, deciding, "Yes, it is worth it and I will do it," or "No, it isn't worth it and I won't do it."

Each time you have a little success, it will make you want to do more. Success feeds on success. Again, the important thing is to be consistent, not to say, "I'm going to devote twenty-four hours this day to getting organized." When you go from one extreme to the other, you are setting yourself up for failure. So be consistent and do a little bit at a time.

One Day at a Time

Part of the task of overcoming inner resistance and getting better organized is learning to set realistic expectations of what you hope to achieve. Since the behaviors involved in being organized are obviously difficult for you (that's why you're reading this book), one of the most important things to strive for in developing organizational skills is to do a little bit on an ongoing basis.

For example, try to set a realistic goal of being organized one day at a time. "Just for today" is an excellent philosophy—not to try to organize your whole life, not to try to organize everything, but *just for today* to try to be as organized as you can. You don't have to resolve all your fears, anxieties, and depression before you begin. Just begin. Often the inner turmoil will lessen as you bring your external environment into a more orderly state.

JUST FOR TODAY

Don't try to take on your whole lifetime and lifestyle, saying, "From now on I'm always going to be organized, all the time, forever, in every aspect of my life." That would be overwhelming. Instead, tell yourself:

- *For this one twenty-four-hour period* I will put things where they belong instead of just tossing them.
- *For this one twenty-four-hour period* I will be on time every place I go.
- *For this one twenty-four-hour period* I will _____. (Fill in the blank.)

Be realistic with others, too. Don't announce to others how organized you're going to become—it may be that your credibility isn't too good! Just let other people see the difference after you've done it. There's nothing more satisfying.

Others' Expectations

When others have unrealistic expectations of us, the result is often resentment. You may be doing your best, but if you're criticized for lack of organization, you may feel resentful.

Suppose there is someone in your life with whom you have a significant relationship who is an Elbie. Let's call her Linda, and let's suppose you find yourself in this position: Linda has many fine qualities, but she can be extremely judgmental and critical, and she has set such unrealistic standards that nobody could live up to them. Maybe you've come to terms with what you can and cannot do, and feel satisfied with your performance, and then Linda comes along and says, "You aren't doing so well on that."

Immediately, feelings of self-doubt may begin to creep in. All the hard work you've done in coming to terms with your own limitations and learning to set realistic expectations may be in jeopardy. At that point it's very important to know that as an adult, the only expectations you need to live up to are your own. We repeat: *The only expectations you need to live up to are your own.* (Also, keep in mind that the kind of criticism that disturbs us most comes when someone says something about us that we fear may be true.)

From time to time you may regress and your confidence may waver. If and when that happens, say to yourself, "I've gotten off my program, but today is a new day. Today I start again."

It's very helpful to know how to cope with others' expectations and criticism; the next chapter will deal with those kinds of conflicts.

SUMMARY

- *Beware of an all-or-nothing working style. Doing a little at a time consistently is the key to success.*
- *Be willing to let go of familiar but ineffective ways of doing things.*
- *Forget "Yeah, but . . ." You can do it!*
- *Replace "should" with "want to" and guilt with action.*
- *Set deadlines for yourself so others don't need to set them for you.*
- *Recognize that conflicts are often within yourself rather than with others.*
- *Learn to set realistic expectations for yourself.*
- *Don't compare yourself with others.*
- *Say the word "oops" when you slip—then focus on what needs to be done.*
- *A cluttered environment may be both the effect and cause of anxiety, making it difficult to focus. You may need to deal with your emotions before you can deal with your clutter.*

14

OPPOSITES ATTRACT

During a workshop, Lori, a spontaneous, gregarious person with a great sense of humor, told a story that summed up the difference between herself and her husband, Larry.

It seems Larry had attempted to instruct Lori on the fact that a potato-chip bag had little tabs at the top, and that those little tabs had a purpose. After a portion of the bag was used, the bag was to be turned down, using those tabs to hold it closed. The lesson didn't get very far before Lori dissolved in laughter.

Lori, of course, couldn't have cared less whether a chip bag was closed, or even if there were ten potato-chip bags open all at once. If she was having fun, something like that would be totally irrelevant—just so *petty* that it would have no significance whatever. Whether the potato-chip bag was open or closed was no big deal—other than that it meant the potato chips might get stale and have to be thrown out.

Fortunately, Lori and her husband were able to maintain a sense of humor in regard to their differences, but not everyone is able to maintain his or her perspective in such a situation. One of the most frequent dilemmas we hear during organizing seminars can be expressed in this type of statement: "My husband is a saver and leaves his stuff all over the house. How can I get him to clean up his stuff?" Both men and women complain almost equally about living or working with partners who "drive them crazy" by being either overly organized or disorganized.

Regardless of their reason for being together, if two individuals don't understand each other and appreciate their differences, problems can and usually do occur. If you have organizational difficulties and you live or work with someone who's very well organized, you probably also experience conflict at times between the two of you.

To Change or Not to Change . . .

If someone were to ask you what problems arise from your lack of organization, you might reply, "I can never find anything when I need it," "I'm always running late," or "It's embarrassing when friends walk into my office and I have papers all over the place." Or you might reply that it's causing problems in your relationship with someone like your parents, manager, teachers, or mate.

Although you may not experience the problem with the disorganization itself, you value the relationship and don't want it to be undermined. You are willing to work on your behavior, therefore, *for the sake of maintaining the relationship.* The only time you can make an inner change, however, is when you *want* to make that change—not because your boss, your parents, your mate, or anyone else wants you to—but because *you* want to.

Pleasing Another Person

There is a definite difference between wanting to change behavior because you value a relationship and wanting to change in order to please another person. At first glance this may seem like splitting hairs, but upon further examination you can understand that there is a basic difference.

People tend to get all tangled up when they feel they are doing something for someone else. If you set out to change a behavior in order to please your spouse, friends, or someone else, you are doing it so *the other person will benefit* and approve of you, and those behavior changes will probably be short-lived.

If you're trying to please others, things may not progress as rapidly as you'd like because the situation becomes one of "tit for tat." You might say, "I'm going to do this for him, and then I'm going to benefit because he's going to do something for me." Or "I'm going to be noble and self-sacrificing and do something for the other person. Then he or she will like me." This kind of motivation isn't sufficient, because it is setting up a parent-child relationship. It's like saying, "I'm going to be a good boy so Mommy will be pleased and approve of me."

On the other hand, of course, if you are continuing in the behavior simply because the other person wants you *not* to, that's the rebellious other side of the same coin. It's still a parent-child type of interaction: "She's not going to tell me what to do. She wants me to clean up, but I'll show her!"

Most people aren't consciously aware of this. They couldn't articulate it, but rather would just have an uncomfortable feeling. If they were to put that feeling into words, they might say, "I don't want to act like a little boy who's trying to please Mommy or Daddy."

Benefits

The bottom line is that whether or not you're willing to change your behavior depends upon how much *you* will benefit. The changes may benefit you directly or they may enhance your relationship—which in turn will benefit you if you value that relationship. The change will probably be difficult. You will only change your behavior if you perceive the long-term benefits to be great enough for you. If not, you'll be reluctant to stick with doing anything different. Only you will know whether or not you consider the benefits to be worth the effort.

Coercion

When you coerce another person into doing what you want, even if you win, you lose. The person may do what you want, but will resent it. In a passive-aggressive way, he or she will probably get back at you in one way or another. Or, somewhere down the line, he or she will sabotage the plan.

Limits Set by Default

Earlier in the book we discussed Arbies' lack of awareness of limits—of time, money, clutter, weight, and so forth. But this tendency of Arbies not to set limits for themselves can hurt their relationships if their partners, by default, end up setting the limits for them—drawing the line and saying, "This is it! The clutter, in addition to being all over the floor in your den, is now overflowing into the living room, and this has got to stop!" At this point they are not engaged in an adult-adult relationship but in a parent-child relationship. The Arbie has placed himself or herself in the position of being either the compliant child who goes along with the limits the mate has set, or the defiant child who refuses to go along with those limits. Either way, the relationship is not one that exists between two adults.

Contradictory Messages

The Elbie partner is likely to be resentful because for him or her it's a no-win situation. The Arbie's message is "Set limits for me because I'm unwilling or unable to set them for myself," but at the same time he or she is saying, "Don't tell me what to do." This often leaves the partner switching back and forth from a hands-off attitude to a disciplinary stance, both without satisfactory results in the relationship.

With this in mind, it's obvious that only when you change behaviors so that *you* can benefit will the changes be long-lasting. If you *want* to change, the first question to consider is "In what way is this behavior causing a problem for me in my daily life?"

Criticism

Let's assume that a person whose relationship you value begins to criticize you. You want to have a good relationship with this person, but at the same time you don't want to change your own style just as a favor to someone else. What is the best approach to handling this dilemma? In dealing with criticism, it's imperative to know how to give it and how to receive it in a way that is enriching to a relationship rather than destructive to it.

Receiving Criticism

Of course, you'll be tempted to respond (as most people do to criticisms of their personal style) by saying, "No, I didn't," or in some other way attempting to negate what the other person has said.

When people are being scolded, they cannot really hear or understand their partner's concern because they feel defensive, so they may laugh or ignore chiding remarks by saying, "That's silly. I can't be bothered," or "What difference does it make?" Or they may become hurt and, in tears, say something like "Oh, you're always picking on me. You're never satisfied. You're always criticizing me," and so on. They may deny the accusation, ignore it, or simply not let it penetrate.

Perceptions

When a person is criticizing you, it's important to know that the person who's doing the criticizing at a particular moment is only expressing his or her own frustration and perception of who you are. One man's colleague at work, for example, will see him in an entirely different way from how he is perceived by his wife and children.

When you are being criticized, concentrate on this question: "Is that what I really am, or is that how this person sees me?" Don't allow another's perception of you to define your self-concept. Once you have understood that the other person only has a different perception, you are in a better position to begin communicating. This may sound simple, but in reality it may take months and months of training to get to that point.

Understanding the Problem

The first goal is to understand the problem. Really listen to what the other person is saying and recognize and understand it as his or her problem. You can then be firm in asserting that he or she owns the problem. What your partner says the problem is, and what is actually bothering him or her, may be two different things. Understanding this is extremely important—so important that we want to address this specific point in greater depth.

Communicating

Your partner may be angry because you've overdrawn the checkbook, put something away in the wrong place, forgotten a deadline, or left the potato-chip bag open. Whatever the reason, if you just zing an angry response back at the other person, it's like starting a tennis match. You find yourself slugging balls back and forth from opposite courts, rather than cooperating with each other.

If, however, you simply don't hit the ball back, you get a different kind of reaction or response. When you let the ball drop and both of you approach the net, that's where communication and cooperation begin. That's why we recommend the following technique:

Whatever the complaint, realize that what your critic is expressing is his or her *perception*. Take ten seconds or so to relax, close your eyes, and step back from your emotions. Renew your feeling of self-confidence and then open your eyes, make eye contact with your critic, and ask calmly and politely, "Would you tell me more about how this is a concern for you?"

Tone of voice is important when you ask about the other person's concerns. If your tone is strained or irritated, of course, you aren't going to get the response you're looking for. You need to show genuine respect for the other person and ask the question with a sincere willingness to listen.

The above question may strike you as silly at first, because you feel that the answers are going to be pretty obvious. However, asking it accomplishes several things: First, it immediately removes *you* from the center of attention and from your need to defend yourself, and it directs the focus *on the other person*. Second, it tends to defuse your partner's anger. Rather than eliciting a rebellious answer, it tends to open the lines of communication on a rational level. Rather than running out of control, emotions and thoughts can then be calmly integrated.

Such a question invites others to share their inner thoughts with you and helps them clarify their own thinking.

Regarding the potato-chip bag, for example, your partner might answer, "It concerns me that we waste so much food around here. I work hard to earn a living, and all our money seems to be frittered away wastefully." What was first posed as an issue of neatness is really a symbol of financial concern. Or your partner might say, "I'm having Ed over to watch the game, and I wanted to serve those chips then. Now there aren't enough."

By using this technique you may learn the person's real concern, which you might not have otherwise understood. By listening openly, you can learn a lot about your partner, thereby increasing the level of intimacy and cooperation in the relationship.

Think about the wonderful benefits of handling criticism in this way. Not only can it help you, but it can also become contagious and "rub off" on people around you.

In an office, managers have an opportunity to set a tone in which differences are handled in a rational manner. It's not only parents, partners, and managers, however, who have this power; anyone, in any setting, can influence others by modeling good communication techniques.

RESPONDING TO CRITICISM

Whenever you are criticized, take a moment to calm yourself, regain confidence, and then respond by saying, "Could you please tell me more about your concern?" It can be a real learning experience.

Clarification

The next step in handling the other person's criticism is to clarify your understanding of the other person's problem. You can reply, "I understand that you are concerned about ——— and that you would like me to ———. Am I hearing you right?" He or she may say, "No, that wasn't really my concern. My concern was ———, and what I would rather you do is ———."

At that point you may realize that your own perception of the other person's problem was faulty and that, had you pursued your own understanding, an argument would no doubt have ensued. Instead, you now know what the person is concerned about, and what he or she would like for you to do.

Resolving the Issue

Does that mean you must do what the other person wants? No. Once you have heard about the other person's concerns, *you have the right and the responsibility to make a choice!* For instance, initially you can respond by saying simply, "Thank you for sharing that with me. I think I understand better now."

Later, when you've had time to reflect on the matter, or have become more skilled in this technique, your response may be "I understand your concern, and yes, this is something I am willing to do." Or it may be "I understand your concern. I am not willing to do ———. However, what I am willing to do is ———."

When you are not willing to comply with the other person's suggestion, be ready to come back with something that will address the person's concerns, but that is within your own realistic expectations of yourself.

Continue on with the discussion at this level until a solution satisfactory to both of you is reached.

Position of Strength

By using this technique, you will no longer feel that you "don't have a leg to stand on," that the other person is "right" and you are "wrong," or that the other person maintains a level of importance superior to you.

When you have realistic expectations of yourself; when you know what's important to you and what isn't; when you feel calm and able to listen to another's concern without having to fight back; when you do not allow another's perception of you to define your self-concept—you are then confident!

This means you are in a *position of strength*. Only when you get to the point where you can respond to criticism from a position of strength can you communicate appropriately.

Let's suppose you have reached the point where you have set reasonable expectations for yourself, and learned not to become upset or to regress or to have self-doubts when someone criticizes you. You are able to stand firm and say within yourself, "I'm satisfied with my own performance." What's the next step?

Giving Criticism

It's equally important to be able to let another person know when something he or she is doing is unacceptable—annoying, inconvenient, inconsiderate—to you.

Suppose, for example, you are reading the newspaper in your nice comfortable chair, having a little snack of a bottle of pop and potato chips (and, of course, you have left the bag open), and you need to get up to answer the phone. When you return, you find your pop bottle has been emptied and put away, your potato chips have been removed, and the newspaper is neatly folded and put in the place the left-brain person has designated for newspapers.

Probably you'd be annoyed. How could you let your partner know how you feel, in a way that would enhance communication?

The first thing to do is *keep the focus on yourself*. (When you are being criticized by another person, keep the focus on the other person. This is the opposite.) In this case the focus needs to remain on you. Recognize and state that you own the problem.

As before, first take a moment to ask yourself, "What is my real concern here?" The concern may be that you feel your partner is too controlling, or that you can never relax when you are around home, or any number of things. How can you approach him or her to make clear that you do not appreciate this left-brain behavior?

You may be likely to get into your feelings right away, responding immediately by wanting to yell. Or, if you are some-what intimidated by your mate, you may go off and sulk. Neither of those approaches, of course, works well.

The need, then, is to verbalize your concern. Once you've gotten your feelings under control (which may take five hours or even five days), let the person know you did not like what he or she did. You can approach your partner and say, "I really feel disturbed [disrespected, put out, not relaxed, uncomfort-able—whatever the feeling is] when I'm in the middle of doing something and I leave for a little while, and then I come back and find you've put all my stuff away."

Then you can tell the person in what way that was a concern for you. It may be that you are working on a project and you have all your books and papers spread out in a certain way. You may then say, "This is a concern for me because when you put my stuff away I can't find anything," or "When you put all my stuff away it takes me an hour and a half to get it all organized again the way I want it so that I can begin my work. When that happens it gives me the impression that you run the show around here and that I don't have equal status in this household. I feel as though it's your house and I can't ever relax and feel comfortable here."

Make a Direct Request

Another way to handle conflict situations, instead of com-plaining, is to *make a direct request.* This kind of directness can work wonders. It clears up so much unnecessary confronta-tion, tension, and stress. One of the authors' children, even, would from time to time respond to his mother in an assertive manner: "Instead of complaining, make a direct request!"

If you're unhappy with something your partner has done, express what you would like him or her to do instead. For example, if your partner has put away a project you had on the dining-room table, you might say, "If the stuff on the dining-room table bothers you so much, what I would like you to do, instead of putting it all away, is take the white linen tablecloth and just lay it on top of all my stuff." Then finish that commu-nication by asking, "Would this be acceptable to you?"

At that point the partner may say, "Yes, that will be acceptable to me. That way all your stuff would be where you want it, but I wouldn't have to look at it every time I walked through the dining room." Or he or she might say, "No, that wouldn't really work for me. I want to be able to use the dining room table. It's a beautiful table, we paid a lot of money for it, I would like to be able to see the surface of it. And it's an eyesore when I walk through there. No, that would not be acceptable to me."

If the partner says it would not be acceptable, then he or she has the responsibility to come up with another solution that would be acceptable. For example, he or she might say, "That would not be acceptable to me. I would prefer, if you are working on a project that you want to leave out all the time, that you leave it out on the Ping-Pong table in the basement. Would that be acceptable to you?"

Then it's up to you to say whether such a solution would or would not be acceptable.

If you say no, however, it is then your responsibility to come back with another suggestion that would be acceptable to you, present that to your mate, and then ask if he or she would find it acceptable.

Keep going back and forth until you come up with something that is acceptable to both of you.

Believe us, this does work. We've seen it work time and again. It may not be ideal from your perspective, in that you may not get everything you want, but it has a very great advantage in preserving the relationship.

It is very possible, given some practice, for a right-brain person and a left-brain person to come up with solutions in a problem-solving situation that they can both live with and say, "Yes, that is within my comfort range. I can live with that." In the meantime, instead of criticizing each other, learn to appreciate your own and others' unique styles. The heart, soul, and core of a healthy adult relationship is mutual decision-making based on nondefensive, confident, good communication that is respectful of both individuals involved.

The actual decisions made are not as important as *how they are made,* because the latter directly affects your relationships and the quality of your life.

SUMMARY

- *Learn to understand and appreciate your partner's style to minimize conflict.*
- *You may wish to modify your own style as another means of lessening conflict in your relationship.*
- *Be a self-starter, so your partner won't have to be a crank!*
- *In a power struggle, even if you win, the relationship loses.*
- *Learn to listen to another's critical perception of you without letting it affect your self-esteem.*
- *Clarify your partner's complaints by asking, "Would you tell me more about how this is a concern for you?"*
- *In conflicts, keep offering alternatives until you find one that is mutually acceptable.*
- *Instead of complaining, make a direct request.*
- *The heart of a healthy relationship is mutual decision-making based on good communication.*

POSTSCRIPT
TO CHAPTER 14

A Word to the Well-Organized Partner of an Arbie:

If you catch yourself asking your mate, child, or colleague, "What's wrong with you? Why can't you get organized?" you might want to consider the difficulties that person is experiencing.

If you read this book carefully, you will understand the depths of the problems incurred by some Arbies—especially if they live or work with someone who, like you, is more highly organized than they.

Viewing life from a right-brain perspective is not wrong, but merely DIFFERENT.

Yes, Arbies *can* change and become more organized, and we certainly encourage them to do so, but *it's much more difficult for them than you can imagine!*

Trying to develop left-brain skills that don't come naturally could be compared to forcing you to tie your right hand behind your back and having to write with your left hand (or the opposite if you are left-handed). You could learn to function pretty normally after a while, but it would never feel right to you. Can you imagine someone criticizing you for not using that arm as skillfully as your naturally dominant one?

Or think of trying to train yourself to pick things up with the other, less dominant hand. You might remember to do it for a time, but after a while you'd tend to forget and return to your more natural way of doing things. Eventually you wouldn't even *think* of using your less dominant arm unless someone reminded you.

This is the way some Arbies feel. Many times, despite their good intentions, they simply don't even *think* to follow left-brain organizational habits, and all the reminders in the world may not change that.

Arbies are sometimes told that they're awkward, stupid, or incapable, and receive all sorts of other putdowns from supposedly well-meaning people. (Occasionally these remarks become verbally abusive, insulting, and totally out of touch with realistic expectations of the Arbie.) These verbal jabs are *always destructive*—both to the Arbie and to the relationship.

Tearing people down is not the way to build them up! Most Arbies really are trying hard to overcome their organizational difficulties, and *they need your understanding and encouragement.* If this situation exists in your family and cannot be remedied using the techniques in this book, *we urgently entreat you both to seek a good counselor* who can help you deal with these issues in an equitable and unemotional manner.

CONCLUSION

The theory of right-brain dominance has helped many people to understand themselves better in terms of their organizational preferences. If you are an Arbie who has been frustrated by trying to fit yourself like a round peg into a square hole in terms of organizing, the techniques in this book have been developed with you in mind.

When you get everything in order, it may seem like a dream come true, and reaching your dreams is what this book is really all about. But remember, they must be *your* dreams—not someone else's. Focusing on your goals can turn your dreams into reality—provided you are willing to work hard. Dedicate your waking hours to this purpose.

Whenever you become aware that you are feeling pressured, stop and examine how you can use your time more effectively. Above all, remember that the purpose of this book is to make your own life more manageable—one step at a time.

If there is an Elbie in your life who could benefit from reading this book, perhaps you would like to set the book out where your partner can see it, opened to the Postscript page.

We recommend beginning to "dig out" right after reading this book—while you are motivated. Your enthusiasm for getting organized may tend to wane as time passes, so this may be the best time to take advantage of your energy.

Even if you forget everything else from this book, please remember this: Designate twenty minutes religiously every single day to putting away clutter. This is only a few minutes in each room or area of your office, but if it is done *every single day,* the results will be truly amazing. It is well worth twenty minutes a day for your own peace of mind.

After reading this book, you may feel you need help implementing its suggestions. Hiring a professional organizer who can facilitate setting up and maintaining a system that will work for you can be a great morale booster. This will assist you in getting past the initial stages and on your way toward getting organized. To find an organizer in your area, contact the National Association of Professional Organizers (NAPO) office in Tucson, Arizona. Each year, NAPO sponsors *Get Organized Week.* This first full week of each October is an excellent time to motivate yourself to reorganize your paper and possessions.

Although a professional organizer may help you in many areas, you may find that you still need to work on self-defeating behaviors and their underlying causes. You may need to deal with such issues as shame, anxiety, and/or depression in order to prevent you from ending up in the same situation all over again. If any of these issues are perpetuating your struggle or are causing you to have conflicts in relationships, you may find it helpful to consult a mental health professional in your locality.

If you would like to share your success stories with us, feel free to write. We'd love to hear from you.

Hang in there—you can do it! We wish you extraordinary success in freeing yourself from disorganization.

BIBLIOGRAPHY

Aslett, Don. *Clutter's Last Stand.* Cincinnati, OH: Writer's Digest Books, 1984.

———. *Is There Life After Housework?* Cincinnati, OH: Writer's Digest Books, 1992.

———. *Who Says It's a Woman's Job to Clean?* Cincinnati, OH: Writer's Digest Books, 1986.

Atkinson, Holly. *Women and Fatigue.* New York: Pocket Books, 1985.

Benson, D. Frank and Eran Zaidel, eds. *The Dual Brain.* New York: The Guilford Press, 1985.

Blakeslee, Thomas R. *The Right Brain.* New York: Berkley Books, 1986.

Burka, Jane B. and Lenora M. Yuen. *Procrastination—Why You Do It, What to Do About It.* Reading, MA: Addison-Wesley, 1984.

Buzan, Tony. *Use Both Sides of Your Brain.* New York: E. P. Dutton, 1983.

Campbell, Jeffrey. *Speed Cleaning.* New York: Dell Publishing, 1991.

Coon, Dennis. *Essentials of Psychology.* St. Paul, MN: West Publishing, 1988.

Covey, Stephen R. *The 7 Habits of Highly Effective People.* New York: Simon and Schuster, 1990.

Culp, Stephanie. *How to Conquer Clutter.* Cincinnati, OH: Writer's Digest Books, 1986.

———. *How to Get Organized When You Don't Have the Time.* Cincinnati, OH: Writer's Digest Books, 1986.

Donahue, Phil. *The Human Animal.* New York: Simon and Schuster, 1985.

Edwards, Betty. *Drawing on the Right Side of the Brain.* Los Angeles: Jeremy P. Tarcher, Inc., 1989.

Felton, Sandra. *Messies Manual.* Old Tappan, NJ: Fleming H. Revell Co., 1983.

———. *Messy No More.* Old Tappan, NJ: Fleming H. Revell Co., 1989.

Fiore, Neil. *The Now Habit.* Los Angeles: Jeremy P. Tarcher, Inc., 1989.

Fulton, Alice, and Pauline Hatch. *It's Here . . . Somewhere.* Cincinnati, OH: Writer's Digest Books, 1986.

Guinness, Alma E., ed. *ABC's of the Human Mind.* Pleasantville, NY: Reader's Digest, 1990.

Hendrick, Lucy. *Five Days to an Organized Life.* New York: Dell Publishing, 1990.

Hemphill, Barbara. *Taming the Paper Tiger.* Washington, DC: Hemphill & Assoc., 1989.

Hooper, Judith and Dick Teresi. *The Three-Pound Universe.* Los Angeles: Jeremy P. Tarcher, Inc., 1986.

Lakein, Alan. *How to Get Control of Your Time and Your Life.* New York: Penguin Books, 1989.

LeBoeuf, Michael. *Working Smart.* New York: Warner Books, 1988.

MacDonald, Gordon. *Ordering Your Private World.* Nashville, TN: Oliver-Nelson Publishers, 1985.

Mayer, Gloria Gilbert. *2001 Hints for Working Mothers.* New York: Quill, 1983.

Mayer, Jeffrey J. *If You Haven't Got the Time to Do it Right, When Will You Find the Time to Do It Over?* New York: Simon and Schuster, 1990.

Mills, Selwyn and Max Weisser. *The Odd Couple Syndrome—Resolving the Neat/Sloppy Dilemma.* Great Neck, NY: Jameison Publishing Co., 1988.

Piel, Jonathan, ed. *The Scientific American (Special Issue): Mind and Brain.* Vol. 267, No. 3. September, 1992.

Restak, Richard M. *The Brain—The Last Frontier.* New York: Warner Books, 1979.

Schlenger, Sunny and Roberta Roesch. *How to Be Organized in Spite of Yourself.* New York: Penguin Books, 1989.

Scott, Dru, Ph.D. *How to Put More Time in Your Life.* New York: Signet Books, 1980.

Silver, Susan. *Organized to Be the Best!* Los Angeles: Adams-Hall Publishing, 1991.

Winston, Stephanie. *Getting Organized.* New York: Warner Books, 1978.

———. *The Organized Executive.* New York: Warner Books, 1985.

Wonder, Jacquelyn and Priscilla Donovan. *Whole Brain Thinking.* New York: Ballantine Books, 1990.

For a complete listing of publications, including audio and videotapes, authored by members of the National Association of Professional Organizers, see *The Educational Resource Dictionary,* published by NAPO and available only from NAPO's office at 655 North Alvernon, Suite 108, Tucson, AZ 85711.

For a "Bibliography on Resources Relevant to Chronic Disorganization," write the National Study Group on Chronic Disorganization, 1142 Chatsworth Drive, Avondale Estates, GA 30002.

INDEX